BACK FROM HELL
AND THE DEVIL DIDN'T WIN

How to Free Yourself from Poverty
and Grow Generational Wealth

Gary M.A. Rahman
Award Winning Author

Back From Hell And The Devil Didn't Win
www.Thedevildidnotwin.com
Copyright © 2018 Gary M. A. Rahman

ISBN-13: 978-1548833848
ISBN-10: 1548833843

Limits of Liability and Disclaimer of Warranty
The author and publisher shall not be liable for your misuse of the enclosed material. This book is strictly for informational and educational purposes only.

Warning – Disclaimer
The purpose of this book is to educate and entertain. The author and/or publisher do not guarantee that anyone following these techniques, suggestions, tips, ideas, or strategies will become successful. The author and/or publisher shall have neither liability nor responsibility to anyone with respect to any loss or damage caused, or alleged to be caused, directly or indirectly by the information contained in this book.

Medical Disclaimer
The medical or health information in this book is provided as an information resource only, and is not to be used or relied on for any diagnostic or treatment purposes. This information is not intended to be patient education, does not create any patient-physician relationship, and should not be used as a substitute for professional diagnosis and treatment.

Publisher
10-10-10 Publishing
Markham, ON
Canada

Printed in The United States of America

Table of Contents

Dedication

The family is the first step toward revolution and an example of self-love. Callie, Kali, Spirit, and my mother Emily Yvonne Gudger, I dedicate this book to you. May we live forever.

Foreword

This is a compelling story of the struggles and triumphs you may face. Gary reminds you that if you challenge yourself to be your best, there will be fire and brimstone. But that is only part of the story. Fortitude is the other part and it brings success with it.

Gary takes you on his childhood journey with detail and color that make *Back From Hell And The Devil Didn't Win* both informative and fun. His transparency is honest and painful, yet giving. He touches on points that will make you look deeply at yourself.

Gary doesn't just talk about his successes; He pulls you into his life of hardship and doubt and shows you how he transformed himself and how you can too. It is rare to find an author who is so blunt and honest about his demons, but Gary does just that. His willingness to share such private struggles in his own life is a testament to his desire for you to win.

This book is a powerful life changer, so I strongly encourage you to read it from cover to cover. Gary has traveled the globe as an investor and radio host. He has met and interviewed millionaires, billionaires and people from every walk of life. He shares secrets of those connections, and sheds light on how you can get out of the rat race. He uncovers the many lies that the devil has told that can keep you as a pawn in the game of life.

No matter where you are in life today, this book can make you better. *Back From Hell And The Devil Didn't Win* is a very well balanced mix of James Baldwin's *Go Tell It On The Mountain* and its storytelling style in addition to how you have an obligation to serve others, Napoleon Hill's *Outwitting The Devil* and how to conquer the devil within you, and Robert Kiyosaki's *Rich Dad Poor Dad* and how to utilize the information age to your advantage.

I got great pleasure from this book, and I believe you will too.

Raymond Aaron
New York Times Bestselling Author

Acknowledgments

As I write this acknowledgment page, there are many people whom I reflect upon, who have been pivotal in my life. Some, I speak of your impact in the body of this book; others, I transfer my love through my energy towards you. I do, however, feel humbled and blessed to thank the Creator of all things but most importantly, for the will. The Creator knows the will is an amazing attribute and I appreciate the gift of a strong will, for it has gotten me through some of the toughest obstacles in my life. Secondly, I want to thank my best friend and greatest cheerleader, my beautiful, intelligent wife Callie. Baby, you pick me up when I'm down and allow me to celebrate every aspect of this journey. Even when I'm in my foolish mind, I give thanks for you. This journey has not been an easy one; but with you, it has been one I would not want to trade. I also want to thank my children: my favorite son, Kali and my favorite daughter, Spirit. It is the love of a parent for their children that motivates them to take on challenges to be their best self and to put them on a better path. You both have inspired me to know my greatest self and to strive for perfection. Always know that Daddy does it all so you can win. I'm your biggest fan. Forever remember these two lessons:

"To whom much is given, much is required."
"Question everything and everybody."

Lastly, I want to acknowledge my universal family. Most of you know who you are without me saying a word. How? Because I probably told you before or we've shared a hug, or a kiss, or a moment. Some of you no longer walk the face of the earth, but you forever live in my heart. It has been your love that has kept me focused, and your commitment that has kept me guided on the right path. For this, I will always be your servant.

I love each of you with all of me.

Chapter 1

Born Winner

"You were born to win. But to be a winner, you must plan to win, prepare to win, and expect to win."

– Zig Ziglar

It all started on an October night, in 1969. There was this woman who had been dating this older man. He was thirteen years older than the woman. He was handsome, with a muscular build, and a strong work ethic. The woman was smitten by the man and even though he was married, she didn't care. The man was extremely attracted to the young woman. She was a fox. I think that was the slang term used back in those days. They had been dating for over a year, and the woman was infatuated.

So, on this October night, she had asked if they could have dinner together. She was a good cook and pretty good company, and like I said, she was a fox, so he was happy to oblige. As the evening progressed, they began to get more comfortable, and proceeded to another part of the apartment; and that is when it happened. This thing that happened had never before happened quite like this. It was dark yet it was very bright. It was damp but very comfortable. There was a buzz that tonight would be a special night. Many even said *"a once in a lifetime moment."* Why was tonight so special? There was nothing special about this night reported on the news. So, what was all the buzz; what was all the fuss about? It was at that moment, when the earth was revolving around the sun, and the moon reflected its glow, that out of nowhere, an explosion occurred that would change the world. Like during any explosion, everything and everyone were moving fast, almost like light speed, but the man and the woman seemed at peace. At that very moment, they seemed not to have a care in the world. It was as if they were in a heavenly state, and their eyes connected like they had never before.

In the dampness of the night, everyone and everything else were moving at lightning speed. Then it happened again; the explosion was even bigger than the first, with light even brighter than what had been seen before, and was different than before. There was an outburst as loud as the sea on the outskirts of the eye of a hurricane. The scream echoed, "It's a miracle! It's a miracle! I've won! I've won! and on August 9, 1970, somewhere in Chicago, the victor revealed himself. When he did, he didn't know that this win would be followed by many losses, and times filled with disappointment and regrets; but for now, he was full, and he was happy.

Visualization or death

When I was in Hell's Kitchen I can remember having great dreams and visualizing my incredible destiny. I didn't know why at the time, but life has shown me why. It was to shield me through the darkness. In my many interviews of other very successful people with similar backgrounds, I have found this to be a common practice. The universe knows our pain and provides the resources we need if we just ask. The same applies for me today. When hit with life's destructing blows, I have tunnel vision, and my goals and dreams become ever present. So much so that I feel like I'm walking the grounds of my three hundred plus acre estate. I will now charge you to visualize. Do whatever is needed that will naturally alter your state until you can realize your dreams. The world is depending on you. Those of us who have been schooled by such powerful life lessons are the key for others on the same road. So, be of service and a good shepherd to those who are lost.

Chapter 2

Star Child

"It's dangerous to be a child star, but it's dangerous to be a child in the ghetto, or to be a child at school being bullied."
– Will.i.am will.i.am

I was born on August 9, 1970, in Chicago, IL, at the University of Chicago Hospital. My parents were the late Emily Gudger and Leon Clemmons. I was born the youngest of five, each parent having two children prior to me.

My childhood was loving but very rough due to the financial struggles of my mother. My mother struggled as a single mother to raise her three children, all while she herself battled with depression. Most of her working years, she would work as a housekeeper or caregiver, but collected welfare most of her life due to her battle with depression. My father was a husband and a hardworking family man who, like many men, liked his *side piece*—one of which was my mother, Emily. Many people spoke well of my father, saying what a good man he was, but I never knew that man. I would see him off and on, or from time to time, but nothing ever consistent. My father would promise to take me to the movies or a ball game, but he would never show, leaving me looking out the window with high hopes and wishes that this day would be different. Those hopes and wishes would end with the setting of another sun, and with me wondering what my father did with his other children.

My mother was always too broke or too tired. So, I would often sit and think about a new day; a time when I would be able to make my own decisions and set my own course. But I had many personal struggles. By the age of ten, my family had moved over a dozen times. We would sometimes only live in a place for three to six months. We transferred from one neighborhood school to the next, and I always needed to adjust to a new teacher, a new set of rules, and a new group of kids. This kept me in a lost state, as if a part of me was dying repeatedly. I was a skinny, soft-spoken child. Like a newly born gazelle in the middle of the jungle, I learned early that I couldn't trust the promise of friendship to protect me from the common certainty of betrayal. It was at O'Keefe School, where I learned life had to get better than this. I struggled daily as the new gazelle, to find my way to get my legs. Many days, I narrowly escaped with my life. So, as any doe would do, I looked to the protection of my mother, and the comfort offered in her care. Folks, I missed forty five days of school that semester alone, and I was reading on a first grade level. I hated school, and I hated my life. I wished, as I talked to the devil, that I would die, and the devil, being true to form, would often tell me how to make that happen.

There was no Christmas that year, and my mom wept. She cried often, but this time was different; it felt as if she was having those same conversations with the devil that I was. I heard her talking about not having the rent again, and this time, no one to bail her out. Shortly after, we would do what we had so often done as a family. We would dance. We would dance to the rhythm of packing boxes and glass dishes being folded within paper for another voyage to tomorrow. This was unlike other times, when an uncle, or Aunt Lizzy or Grand Mommy, would save the day. This time, the sheriff was scheduled for the following day. As I carried black garbage bags full of clothing and other items out of the apartment, I made a promise to myself. I made a covenant that one day I would be a millionaire, and this would never happen to me and my family. Understand, at the time, I did not know how big the promise, or the size of the obstacles I would have to climb. I remember feeling sick to my stomach, but I also felt like, perhaps, I got a little payback against the devil for what he said to me, and what I believe he said to my mother.

A couple of years went by with not much change: we moved; I transferred; we moved again. It was a new day, and this time I was on my own. My sister, Susan, had graduated and gone off to high school. My new school, this time, was at least in a familiar neighborhood. I had grown up knowing some of the children because the school was in the neighborhood where my grandmother lived, and our family church was there too. Unlike the other schools, where I felt the teachers ignored me, or pretty much acted as if I didn't exist, this place was different. Teachers, at the other schools, knowing I couldn't read, would skip past me, taking me off the hook; and I would be relieved not to have the pressure. So, at 12 years old, I entered Arthur Dixon School, reading on the third grade level. I was assigned to Ms. Valentine's class. Ms. Valentine was a tall woman with a dark complexion. She had an Afro and a strong personality. You could tell, however, that when she was young, she was a nice looking woman. Ms. Valentine didn't take any stuff—she frightened me; she frightened all of us. I complained often to my mother that she was mean. If you talked, she would hit you with a ruler or scream and throw erasers and chalk at you. She never threw anything at me, but she screamed a lot, and I did get the ruler. But what I hated about her most of all was that she never skipped me during reading. She would make me struggle to pronounce each word. She would ensure that I got what I call a stinky shower every day, from my sweat that drenched me as it ran down my face and back in a pool of embarrassment.

It didn't seem to stop with her. I was both fortunate and cursed, all at the same time. One of the first mentors and father figures in my life was the late Pastor Kenneth

Corby. Pastor Corby was my first real encounter with someone of non-African origin. Well, I had white teachers in school, but up until Pastor Corby and my aunt through marriage, I had an all-black world. Pastor Corby pushed me beyond myself. He accepted no excuses for failure due to mediocrity, and he always told me I was a gift and that I had purpose. I sometimes don't know who was harder on me, Pastor Corby or Ms. Valentine; they both made me measure myself. By the end of that school year, I had gone up more than three levels in both reading and math. I had the devil on the run.

Arthur Dixon School was like that; and the teachers could get the best out of all their students. All my friends that I grew up with in the neighborhood were all excellent students. I was the runt of the litter. Understand that today's prison system is designed to house future generations of children just like me: black males being raised by a stressed out mom, living below poverty, with no real direction or future. By the age of eleven, the system has determined their future and in which direction they will go. The good money is usually against a positive outcome. (When gambling the odd favorite is also called the good money)

With all the shortcomings of my beautiful and loving mother, one strong point was her belief in her children.

She never graduated from high school, but she believed that her children could do anything they wanted to, and she made me a believer. She could tell a story that would keep you at the edge of your seat. I recall her often telling us that if you ever wanted to visit a place, read about it and learn about it, and it would be like being there. So, I grew up visiting the museums. They were free, and I could dream. My mother was special, and I always felt her love. One day, I was struggling to make peace with the feeling that I was a mistake. Why was I born? My father had hoped that my mother would have aborted me. I know, that having me added more difficulties on an already overly stressed situation. I recall being about nine, and my mom had gotten a really nice apartment; it had three bedrooms, and the building was well maintained. It was during a time in our history as a nation when you could discriminate against children. The building had a *no children* policy. There were places that would take pets before they would take children. It reminds me of today, when I hear people advocating on behalf of animals before standing up for human rights of people. Well, anyway, my mom got the place because she told the management that her children were older. She said her son was a teenager and her daughter was twelve. She had to leave me off the rental agreement because a nine-year-old would have surely caused her to be denied tenancy. She explained the situation to me and my siblings, and we liked the place so much; we felt it was worth the risk. So, I walked gingerly, as a gazelle would do, and I lived as quietly as a mouse—as quiet as a nine year old could. The neighbors would peek out their windows, hoping to get a glimpse of the young doe. After only a few months, this dream quickly turned into a nightmare. The tenants had complained that the new lady had a young child in apartment three; therefore, the relocation plan was in full preparation. There was only one last thing for a nine-year-old to do, and that was to sit God down for a talking to. I carried a picture in my pocket of who I thought Jesus was: a blue-eyed, blonde guy. You know the picture—the one that Leonardo Da Vinci painted. I pulled that picture out of my pocket, and I told that Jesus a thing or two. I let it all fly; I got it all off my chest: "Jesus, you disappointed me. After all this belief, and you turn out to be fake." I remembered crying so hard, as I tore that picture of *Jesus* apart and threw it in the toilet. The devil told me to flush, but the little church boy didn't have it in him. I put my hand in the toilet and pulled Jesus out before the devil made me change my mind. You know, that devil is slicker than a ballroom floor, fresh on Saturday morning, or some might say, a preacher on Sunday morning. If you're not careful, he will surely get his way. Napoleon Hill should have taught us that. I wasn't convinced until my loving mother asked me if I wouldn't mind living with my Grandmommy. It hadn't dawned on me, until that moment, that maybe I was the issue. Maybe I was the reason we did not have a stable home. So, a few years later, I remember asking my mother, after hearing her argue with my father, if I was a mistake. She tried her best to assure me that I was not, but I still had my doubts. So, I told Pastor how I felt, and only like Pastor Corby could, he yelled at me and told me I was God's child first, and God didn't make mistakes. Was this the same God I had been so disappointed in? I wondered and I struggled; I even shared my feelings with my Special Ed teacher, Mrs. B Haynes. She also told me I was not a mistake, but I was still not completely convinced. You see, at that time, all I had was heartache. All I really knew well was disappointment—not just my own but my family's too. I made that promise to myself back when I was ten—do you remember that promise?—I was never going to let my life reflect the one my mother's did: I was going to be a millionaire. That being said, the devil was still ever present. I needed a win. I needed it now.

So, on a sunny June afternoon, the party was on. It was the end of the school year jam: time to celebrate our year of success and our new journeys ahead. I had, for many years, entertained my family with my dancing at cookouts and other family functions. Today was the day I took my act on the road. I struck up the nerve that when the right song came on, I was going to steal the show. My mom called me her star child, and today was the day I let Ms. Valentine's sixth grade class know. So, after the first round of hotdogs and chips, the master began to play. You ask who the master is. Well, in 1983, his name was Michael—Michael Jackson—and the song was Billy Jean. I had performed Billie Jean many times in front of family, but never like this. I was possessed: if you could have seen it, you would have thought, if only for a second, that Michael was paying a visit to Ms.Valentine's class. The room of children erupted with cheers and celebration. The energy was amazing, and everyone was shocked to see this side of me. Little did they know, this had only scratched the surface of things to come. The star child had given the children of Arthur Dixon a glimpse of his power.

Over the following two years, I continued to display my power. With my direction, I helped a good friend of mine become class president, against what many thought were incredible odds, but I unconsciously knew something they didn't. Unknowingly, I had begun to learn how to outwit the devil. You see, over seventy years ago, Napoleon Hill wrote that he had broken the devil's code. The code was so controversial that Hill's family just recently shared the story about the code, revealing them to the world. I, however, was doing some code breaking, with limited understanding, if any, on how to do so.

My last year at Dixon proved to be life changing, and the win I needed. It seemed to be my year. My teachers picked me to do every speaking part at every event they had. They had been so impressed with my previous two performances, that I now was *Mr. Go To*. I loved it. It seemed to feed my spirit like nothing ever before. So, for graduation, I was asked to write a speech. It was such an honor and a boost of confidence, and I went right to work. For so many years at those other schools, the teachers would ignore me, but now I was the man. I had true and loyal friendships, many that have lasted until today. Two of my classmates were the best men in Callie's and my wedding, and a third was a groomsman. These types of real connections had never happened before, and I was no longer a gazelle—I was a lion. On that sunshiny day in June, everyone in the auditorium heard me roar. There were other students who had speeches, but everyone—and I mean everyone— liked mine the best, so much so that people were excited that they were there to meet me and to know me. After the ceremonies, as I prepared to leave the building, my home room teacher, Mrs. Nettles, pulled me aside. Beaming with a smile so bright that I nearly needed sunglasses to make eye contact with her, she made a statement I will never forget. "I am going to read about you. You are going to be somebody." I hugged her and thanked her, and I knew she was right. I have never again felt like I was a mistake. At that very moment, I had forgiven my father for not being a dad, and all the teachers, prior to Ms. Valentine, who never showed a vested interested in me. They were all forgiven, and I had the devil on the run.

Change how you see yourself

My daughter Spirit is a beautiful eight year old with a smile that lights up a room. People are drawn to her first because of I believe her powerful name. Thanks to my wife, she has a name that literally means breath of God. I chose her middle name after my idol, Ali, which means the greatest. So there you have it; she is the greatest of God's breaths. Can you imagine going through life with people looking at you in reverence just because of your name? Well, it doesn't matter how others see you if you don't see yourself in your greatness first. You must find value in yourself before anyone can see value in you. Know that God doesn't make mistakes, nor did he create any of us to be at the bottom rung. I know you might feel like God has forgotten about you or that you don't matter, but the truth is, only a diamond can withstand the pressures of the earth. You were made to be great; you just haven't discovered who you are, and you may have allowed those who hate you to define you. When my daughter argues with her brother Kali, he seems to get the best of her when he says something mean about her. So, my wife and I are constantly reaffirming what a beautiful and intelligent little girl she is, and we stress the importance of not allowing anyone to have such power over her. She is powerful no matter what others may say. The same is true for all of us, so don't be an eight year old. Change how you see yourself.

Know your worth

Being the product of an affair and not really having a relationship with my father, for many years I questioned my worth. I wondered why I was born and can remember having suicidal thoughts as young as nine years old. I always had people around me that loved and cared for me, so I can only imagine children that are left to raise themselves. I'm sure it can be tough.

I have a friend, Darnell. I am sure he wouldn't mind me sharing his story because it was one that he shared when he was a guest on my radio show Connection. Darnell is the oldest of five. We grew up together in Chicago. We ran high school track together and shared and supported each other in our struggles. Darnell's mother was addicted to drugs, and his father was absent from the home. Darnell grew up with a lot of hurt and questions about why he was left to raise his four younger siblings. He and his siblings lived in an abandoned building in the middle of Chicago's bitter cold winters. He shared that they would sometimes use water from the fire hydrant to wash themselves for school. They missed meals and often were left uncared for and unsupervised. Today, however, Darnell has a loving wife, Ann. He is a proud father and owner of several businesses. I like sharing his story because Darnell and his siblings are all homeowners with families of their own. As children they didn't have much, but Darnell knew his value was not defined by what he wore on his back or where he lived, but it was inside him. He knew his worth. I pray you know yours. Darnell has since impacted the lives of many: as a health coach, school owner, father and husband. I wouldn't want to imagine life's void without his impact. Know your worth.

Chapter 3

A Jock's Life

"I hate every minute of training, but I said, 'Don't quit. Suffer now and live the rest of your life as a champion.'"
– Muhammad Ali

The second biggest, they called it. I did not know how to describe it, but yes, I knew it was big. I might have even sometimes called it huge. Others admired it because of its size. It was hard to keep clean, and sometimes hard to wrap your head around why it was so big. What was the purpose for its size? Its correct name was Chicago Vocational High School, but most knew it as CVS, or *Crime, Violence, and Sex*. It became my first training ground into manhood. As a freshman, the first day of school was overwhelming, to say the least. This place was massive, and it had over 4000 students. Those are small college numbers, not high school. I needed to find a security blanket of some sort so not to get lost in the shuffle. I always wanted to play football and wrestle. I had never played organized ball, and I was so skinny that I decided to defer that option for a couple years. I never wrestled, but to this day, I'm not sure why not. I've been a martial artist for much of my life. I love the contact and the self determination that it fosters; but instead, I decided I would try the track team. At the time, I convinced myself that I was doing it to build up my speed for football. I joined during the cross country season. Some call that the worst time to be involved in a track program. Especially in a city like Chicago during the fall and winter. I trained for hours after school in the blistering cold. If my coach said to run five miles to warm up, I did it with no questions and no back talk. When she said to run ten miles, I faced the challenge with an attitude of accomplishment. To me, it was already done; I just had to put in the work. Time after time, and day after day, that is what I did. I did it so much and so well that I was asked to join the varsity cross-country team in my sophomore year. It was a great feeling of accomplishment when I received my varsity letters. The track team had become my security blanket at this massive school called CVS. I had instant friends and family whom I still keep in touch with to this day. During those three years of track, I learned a lot about myself. I learned that, over my short life, I had become a hard worker. It also taught me that often times what you put into something is what you get out. I was determined to give it all that I had, and for three years, that is what I did.

Then, I met her. To me, she was beautiful; her smile and laugh could fill a room. She was sweet and soft spoken, and I loved it. Her name was Yolanda, and she and I spent the last two years of high school supporting and challenging one another to be our best academically. I think it was that relationship with Yolanda that helped

me appreciate the value of a good woman. Before her, I was at best a C student, just keeping my grades good enough to run. She was at a better school and was a solid B student. I did not want to be a slacker, so I began to focus more on my books, and less and less on sports. It probably didn't help my sports career that she also smelled better and was soft. My grades skyrocketed and, as a junior, I recalled the ten-year-old who couldn't read: he was now making the honor roll. My coach was happy to see my grades improve, but she was disappointed that I was not focused like I once was on my training. She threatened to kick me off the team. In my last track meet, I came in dead last. I even got lapped, but I continued to run. The people in the stands laughed, but I ran. My coaches said stop, but I ran. You see, I had learned more at that point than my coaches or the people in the stands, I had learned that I wasn't losing—I was winning. My reading, my grades, and my self-confidence had never been higher. This track meet was probably my last and my final run, and I was going to finish, whether they liked it or not. I finished in last place with my head held high, and I no longer needed this security blanket. I had learned something big about myself, and it was bigger than any medal I could have received on that day.

I continued to stay focused on my academics. Being that I was a junior, there was no better person to encourage this than my shop teacher and father figure, Mr. Rodney Walker. It was sheet metal shop, and my high school major. I had made a decision between majoring in sheet metal and architectural drafting. You see, when I was ten, I also said I wanted to be an architect. Well, I really enjoyed both programs and had a fondness for both teachers, but Mr. Walker was special. He connected with his students in a way that we just knew he loved each of us. He also knew how to get the most out of each of us. So, when I decided on sheet metal, I weighed the pros and cons. Sheet metal had some drafting and all the guidance of Mr. Walker. I chose Walker. In those last two years, he challenged us to grow not only as students but as men. He made us take responsibility for our actions or lack thereof. He was a family man, and he shared his love for his family with us. I know that listening to him also made me want to be a great father, husband, and role model. He had his own business, and many of his best students work on jobs with him. He paid us a man's wage, and when I visit Chicago, there are buildings to this day, that I point out to my family with pride, because I worked on them. He helped me become one of the best students in sheet metal, in the state of Illinois. So, as a senior in high school, I had work displayed at the Museum of Science and Industry—talk about a dream fulfilled!

I was fortunate to have some great men in my life. My Uncle J was another one, and he knew me well. We spent a lot of time together. When I was at my slick age of fourteen, he would "check me" and teach me a lesson on character. Those lessons paid off because it really became a part of how I viewed the world. Better yet, it was how I wanted to change the world. I always had a deep affection for black people. I never knew, nor do I know now, from where it fueled, but I grew more and more intrigued. That affection made me take notice of all types of things: politics, black on black crime, and sex, to name a few. I recall the election of Harold Washington for Mayor of Chicago. It was the first time I had ever seen a black person run for such a high office, but that was not my biggest takeaway: Harold

Washington's energy, and his commitment to his people, was the most meaningful takeaway for me. This town had seemed to always keep its foot on a brother's neck. Good times were never really good at all. I mean, really, who wants to be "scratchin' and surviving". That is not good times. My family's life played this song on a daily basis, so to see a man like Mayor Washington, leveling the field of play, was refreshing. I helped in his campaign, and the buzz in the city was electrifying. The night he was elected, the city's south side erupted, and we all experienced what a good time should really feel like.

Chicago was always political and had some of the most controversial figures in the nation. People like Muhammad Ali and Elijah Muhammad were an everyday presence to Chicagoans. The pride for self that Ali modeled was spiritual for me. I loved this man. His fast talk, his unyielding will in the ring, and his uncompromising will outside the ring made me want to be just like him. I studied the man, and still do. So, on that Sunday in church, when Pastor Corby spoke unkindly of him and Elijah Muhammad, it didn't go over easy with me. Remember how I said I loved Pastor Corby. He was a huge part of who I was becoming as a young man, but oddly, not that part. I was hot. How dare he speak of my idol in such a demeaning way. I didn't even really know much about Elijah Muhammad, but that sermon on that Sunday made me go and research. Why was Pastor so against such men like Ali and Elijah? They were both well respected on the south side, much like Harold Washington. They built pride in a people that were constantly being knocked down. It was maybe that search for more knowledge of these two men that began my love for reading. The more I read, the more people it led me to: Malcolm X, Frederick Douglass, Mary McLeod Bethune, and a host of others. I became so fascinated by the many accomplishments of black people, and I would share stories at school. Once, as a writer on the school newspaper, I wrote a controversial article about gangs. The title was *Gangs Equals Cowards*. In the second largest school in the city and known for its share of gang violence, many people thought I had gone *rabid* to speak so boldly about such a subject. It never even dawned on me that I would get such a response. I stood so strongly on the subject; I believe it garnered me more respect from my peers. Children at school began to call me *young Malcolm*. I loved it so much, I bought prescription glasses similar to his. It didn't stop there with the articles. I took my beliefs and convictions to the street. One day, as I was returning home from school, at the ripe age of sixteen, I saw a strange man beating on his lady friend. This guy had the look of a guy just out of jail and no one came to pick him up. When I intervened, just after he gave the woman a *two piece* upside her head, I looked him dead in the eye, and said, "Hey brother, you are not going to beat on this sister like that, out in these streets, in front of all these children." The look in his eyes were those of a dead man walking. He looked straight through me as if he was trying to see my soul. He must have; he stopped and stared at me for a while as if he saw the Almighty himself. It was during this time the woman was able to get away. I was fearless and nothing like that was going to take place on my watch. Not on my post. When I shared that story with my mother, she, too, thought I had gone *rabid*. My response to her was, *"Someone has to stand up for our people. Why not me?"* It was these experiences that led me to realize that fear was man's imagination playing a trick on him. It was made up, whether it be the fear of the unknown, or whether we create our own prejudices, that feed our races or inhumane behavior. It's our own fear that haunts us, and I refused to let fear get the best of me.

I became a student of history. I wanted to study everything I could get my hands on. I read James Baldwin and the autobiography of Malcolm X. I studied Frederick Douglass, Mary McLeod Bethune, and a host of blacks in history. I listened to hours of the Last Poets and Louis Farrakhan records. I was understanding and appreciating myself and my history on such a level that it frightened my own mother. She felt I was becoming too black. Can you imagine being black, hoping your family would be excited to learn of their greatness, only to be met with resistance and fear? My mother, who had grown up in the church, felt my study of history was a betrayal to my faith. I have learned over the years that many black people feel this way. Perhaps colonialism subconsciously poisons black people to a point that they grow a fear of questioning the many lies. If so, I had an antidote, and it was truth. I began to question and challenge all that I had been told, and no one, and nothing, was going to change my new reality—not even the love I had for my mother. Definiteness of purpose was growing inside me, and the devil was beginning to take notice that he might have a problem; but he was far from done with me, and I was just getting started.

It was 1990, and I had completed my first year of college, but it seemed the real knowledge was back at home the entire time. I had been indirectly getting schooled but had not gone to hear for myself. Well, that day would be the day when all that changed. My best friend's parents were Muslim, and midway through my freshman year, I too had made my *Shahada*. I had changed my name to Habeallah, (which means friend and lover of Allah), and was walking in the footsteps of one of my idols, El Hajj Malik El Shabazz, also known as Malcolm X. Something didn't seem right with the way I had converted. It appeared I had missed a pivotal step, and now I was to complete it. I woke up excited, and once I arrived at my destination, I instantly knew why. It was a grand place, and the most beautiful place I had ever been inside. The people looked better than any I had ever seen. I mean, the women had an aura of beauty that I had never experienced, and the men glowed with a confidence that inspired me to want to raise my game. I had heard this place was a reformer of women and men, but this was more than I expected. The place was orderly, and members were not only polite but they all seemed royal. I could only think back to the description I read about the Messenger as James Baldwin painted him and the believers in *The Fire Next Time.* Each speaker was powerful, and their message was uplifting, one after the next: men, women, and even young ministers younger than myself at the age of nineteen. I was blown away. Then, he appeared: the man of the hour; the man I had been listening to for so many years. This was the man so many hated, yet so many loved. He had been called an anti-Semite by many Jews, and a hate monger by many whites, and black Christians just simply didn't want anything to do with the man and his message. I wanted to know why so many disliked him and his teacher Elijah Muhammad. How could a man be both hated and loved with as much passion as both sides displayed? I was about to find out live and direct. As Minister Louis Farrakhan spoke on that Sunday afternoon in August, I was glued to my seat. I wanted to hear with understanding. I watched everything that day and, by the end of his lecture, I felt charged to create change—change in myself and in my community—and I have never looked back. I wanted to become a registered member, but prior to that decision, I had made another. I had recently enlisted in the army to assist with paying for college. I didn't know at the time that both of these decisions would be like trying to mix oil and water. I shared my dilemma with the sister over new registrars at Mosque Mariam, and she said, "Brother, you can't do both. The Nation of Islam doesn't allow active military to become members." I was shocked and disappointed but understood. How could I serve in a military that was engaged in war crimes around the world, and be a voice and agent for justice for those same people? All I knew was I had to get out somehow. I told my army recruiter that I was a conscientious objector, and he said that it was fine. He told me there were others. So, despite my attempts, I was on my way to be all that I could be, in an army that hadn't wanted black people to be very much. So, a few weeks later, I showed up to swear my oath. The first time I did it, I faked it; I couldn't bear to say the words. What was I doing here? I stood and thought to myself, "I am a freedom fighter, not a pawn for colonialism." As I stood there, faking it, the sergeant locked eyes with me and made me repeat it after him. I repeated the oath and was on my way to a life that would forever keep me driven.

I arrived in Fort Sill, Oklahoma, on August 19, 1990. I was committed to not letting them break me. I would show them that not only was I mentally strong, I was physically superior. For the next eight weeks, I did just that. I ran so well, they made me a road guard. I was lean, I was strong, and I was a protector. Things were starting to get heated in Kuwait as the US and Iraq could not come to terms. Now, here I am, a Muslim in the US army, preparing to fight in a war against other Muslims. This was not the person I wanted to be. My idol, Ali would not stand and recite an oath that colonized the disenfranchised, and say nothing about training to kill them. I had to do something fast if I was ever going to be able to live with myself. I knew I would come under hard criticism from the military elites, but I had to put a stop to my involvement. So, I asked to speak to my drill sergeant in private. I told him I was a conscientious objector and that the white man was the *devil. (I don't have these same sentiments today but at twenty in this country I found it justified by the treatment black people suffered.)* Can you imagine my drill sergeant's face? He knew I was serious, but I think he was also hoping they wouldn't break me. He escorted me down to meet with the First Sergeant a day or so later. I recall it like entering the devil's den: nothing but stripes and high ranking brass with about seven men in total. My drill sergeant wasn't in the office, but there was a black sergeant sitting on a couch. I was asked to explain my request for an early discharge on the base of a conscientious objector. Everything was going smoothly, or so it seemed. After my remarks, the office erupted with yells of fury. The men were all over me. I could smell what they ate for dinner the week prior, they were so into my space. They called me everything but the son of God, and threatened to do all sorts of bodily harm. I, however, showed no sign of fear or weakness; after a while, the room began to calm. The black sergeant who was sitting on the couch never said a word, but in the most unsettled way, his face said, "That a boy." I had gotten these men off- balanced. Image that, some of the most battle-trained men in America's Army were dismayed by my conviction and fearlessness, so much so that they honored my request to speak to the first officer. I continued my training as I awaited my next meeting. I saw black soldiers being mistreated by white sergeants, and I requested to be their mentor. You see, I was leveraging the relationship I had with my drill sergeants—two black and one Asian. I requested to mentor a guy I noticed having a hard time in another platoon. So my drill sergeant, simply because of my request, had the guy moved to his platoon. I must admit, this had to be guided by a higher power; as I am writing this, I almost find it to be unbelievable, but I was there. I took the kid under my wing. He was moved to a nearby bunk, and I coached him through a rough patch. I think they had gotten in his head, and he was what they called *8 up*, meaning he could do nothing right. His punishment for this was extra push-ups or holding an eighty-pound bullet until he cried. They felt breaking him down was the best way to make him better. It wasn't working; it had been weeks and he was still making the same mistakes. I didn't like what I was seeing, and I simply asked if he could be moved to our platoon. My sergeants, I believed, respected me, but they couldn't say it with words, so they went to bat for me in ways like this. I think, deep down, they knew I was right about some of the other things I shared; like how this country continues to lie about democracy, equality, and justice for all, while still not providing equality in its own country to its own citizens. I shared these feelings with others in my platoon, and they also took notice of how I handle myself. I was a young man just trying to make a way for myself, but, to the best of my ability, I completed every task. They knew I was just there to earn money to finish school. Each Sunday, I went to the mosque; and almost every Sunday, someone I knew wanted to attend with me. The Imam was amazed by how many people came back with me each week. One Sunday, he told me, I was special. Since the time he had taken on the post of Imam, he had never had such a turnout. I was pleased to hear it, but I knew that there was something different about me, and about how others were drawn to me. I felt very powerful, but in a serving kind of way. My words were my bond, and

I was willing to carry all the weak to the finish line. After my meeting with the first officer, I was told what to do in order to be discharged, and I began working on it. The first officer asked me if I thought I could finish my training, and I answered, emphatically, yes! By the end, I was glad I had because there were others who couldn't continue, and were still there with no end in sight. As I continued with the next part of my training, my new sergeant was the great grandson of Robert E. Lee. He was a piece of work, and we butted heads until the very end. He could see early on that I was a leader, and appointed me line captain. He gave me all of his headaches and tried to break me by giving me power over men. I didn't fall for his manipulation—I stepped down after only a week. He knew about my views, and he hated my pride, but I stayed focused and finished that training too. I returned to Tuskegee University in the fall with an energy that I would work hardest for myself. You see, for four months, I felt what it was like to be told what to do. Now, I had the choice of doing what I wanted. In the army, I had to get up at 4:30 am for PT (physical training), so to get up by 6:00 am to prepare for class was easy. When I returned to school and called my local army base about my GI bill, they told me they had never heard of such a thing. I guessed I must have really pissed some folks off; I always believed my record was marked. I served honorably until my unit closed due to cutbacks, and they asked for volunteers for early outs. I could now become a registered member of the Nation Islam, and I couldn't wait.

That summer I stuck around school to work and attend summer school. The next year, I pledged Kappa Alpha Psi. (A college fraternity) It had been a wish of mine since I was told about the great men at the age of fourteen. The brothers of Gamma Epsilon made a big impression upon me, and my pledged program was one I appreciate to this day. I will speak more about this later because it has been one of my best decisions and has added to my success.

The following summer: I returned home to Chicago as a Kappa, and now it was time to finalize my registration as an F.O.I., better known in the Nation of Islam as the Fruit of Islam. Why? Because a tree is known by the fruit it bears. I was assigned to arguably the greatest squad in the history of the Nation of Islam; the Task Force. We were given the hardest tasks, and we stepped up to every challenge. Many of these men were some of the greatest I had ever known. Most were filled with a love for themselves and a great love for their people. The average age of the men was something like twenty. It was hard to believe, we were so young and so focused on achieving greatness. One brother, whom I will always remember, was Brother Aaron Muhammad. He had an amazing spirit. I have never been one to put anyone on a pedestal, but I felt at the time that I would follow this brother to the end of the earth. He was second in command of the Task Force, and Minister Farrakhan's godson. First in command Prince Akeem was another story (quite different from Arron). He had a dark side to him. One I could not put my hands on, but I sensed that he was different than the others. He had the blessings from Minister Farrakhan to lead the men of the Task Force, and he seemed to do that well. I heard he had once been the leader of one of Chicago's street gangs. They said he was nice with his hands, meaning he could fight. He walked around with a confidence that I guess helped him in leading men, but he and I never really got along. I have never been one to take orders well, especially when I didn't feel the person was genuine. He had rubbed me the wrong way from the very beginning. When I arrived back from school for the summer I was focused on finishing what I had started before going into the army. I also wanted to serve my community. The teachings of Elijah Muhammad had been life-changing for many, and I was there to do my part which was moving us a bit further. Prince Akeem seemed to like power and followers. He was a rapper and had established some fame. Several big name artists like Chuck D and Ice Cube were in his circle, but these things didn't mean much to me. Since I didn't seem to be a groupie or one looking for his approval, he would be a bit condescending when speaking to me. He referred to me as "College Boy." I found this odd because ninety percent of all the men in the Task Force were college students. He was demanding and I was cool with that as long as it pertained to what we called, at the time, Nation business (work that was important to serve the greater community). With his leadership the Task Force held the record for most Final Call Newspapers ever sold by one squad in a twenty-four hour period. We did that and a host of other things that gave us *go where we want, do what we please* privileges. This would later be the very reason for its downfall.

Being in the Task Force made all of us in it feel a certain pride and privilege because of all our hard work. Whenever called on we could and would step up to any task. The others members in the nation, both men and women, respected us for our dedication. We were known as the benchmark of the FOI. We escorted celebrities and went on almost all high detail jobs. We trained, we ate, we practically lived at the mosque. I can honestly say I spent six days or nights of the week there. Which brings me to that Friday night in August. I had not spent time with my childhood friend since returning home from college. Friday's brothers rarely showed and I needed a break. So, I decided to hang, laugh and be silly with some of my best friends that night. Things were going great until we came out of a restaurant and walked right into Prince Akeem and some other members of the Task Force. The one night I chose not to go to the mosque was the one night Prince Akeem would be at the same place I was. He was not happy with me and said he wanted to see me in the ring later in the week. As I said earlier, he was good with his hands, and had intimidated other brothers with this threat before, but I was cool with seeing what he could do. He never showed to the ring and I'm not sure he ever intended on being there, but he liked to strike fear in those he could. It didn't work with me, but that wasn't the last time he tried.

The Task Force had a motto: *Whatever was asked, it ain't nothing but a task.* It is a motto I still live by today. Most of the brothers in the Task Force are still doing great things today for the improvement of black people and the world as a whole. Many are no longer directly affiliated with the Nation of Islam, but most credit the teachings for a part of their success. Unfortunately,

Brother Arron is one of a few who are no longer here with us, but his spirit lives on in many of our hearts.

The Nation gave me purposeful direction and was a consistent reminder that the struggle for justice is long and humbling. The level of love one must have for himself and his people must be too large to measure in order not to tire and to be a servant. In 1992, I was given the mane Muhammad, by Minister Farrakhan and I learned that I too was worthy to be praised. I have vowed to live up to the call of serving the people, and I pray to leave a legacy of doing this for generations to come, for *life ain't nothing but a task.*

The Task Force was disbanded because it was later discovered that Prince Akeem had been turning brothers out. Several of the members had been having sex with him. Some were embarrassed, one I knew later died of aids, and I knew one even hung himself in his dorm room while wearing a Prince Akeem shirt. The power we had, and more importantly the power he had, went unchecked for so long that it was too long. A lot of promising young men never got to hit their peak. Minister Farrakhan was deeply affected. I think we all were. It was shocking and maturing for me. I never looked at leadership the same way again, and I never took being a good leader lightly.

Being in the Nation, I experienced a lot of life-changing events; most good but some have given me a thicker skin and a better understanding of group dynamics. Some were hard to deal with, but I would not change a thing. One thing Akeem affirmed for me is that when your spirit speaks to you about a person, you need to listen.

Chapter 4

I'm the Teacher

"I spent countless hours listening to my college business professor tell the class how to write a business plan. He would tell us how to operate a business, with talk about supply and demand, only to discover that I was the one person in the class to successfully own and operate a real business. I have always struggled with those in authority or 'experts' who didn't follow their own advice."
– Gary Rahman, Teacher

I had always heard of this place. Its rich history is the true essence of America, but to be here and to walk on the same grounds of such great men and women was surreal. All of the inventions and great discoveries made on these grounds have only paved a path for me. This great place, with great minds, is a true example of building foundations of self-reliance, brick by brick. It seemed to be a perfect choice for me. I thought of the many who had trained here, being pioneers, and many being the greatest at what they did; and in many cases, having been the first and only. It was hard to believe that, in this little town, such greatness was achieved. This place didn't even have a major supermarket, and the people seemed a bit backwards. I soon found out that many of these people would help develop me and would become some of my most admired people. I was now a student at the illustrious Tuskegee University.

My first days were magical. I had never flown on a plane or travel more than a few hundred miles from home. To be on my own, setting my own trail, was exhilarating. I enrolled in the school of architecture, and I was ready to show them my star power.

I quickly realized that my biggest challenge would not be the difficulty of the work, but the control of the instructors. I see why so many of our greatest inventors and entrepreneurs dropped out of college. That title of instructor took on new meaning for me. Here I was, a young man who, a year prior, had work displayed in the Museum of Science and Industry and on buildings where I had done major work. Now, I was being told by my instructor, if I miss more than three days of class, it would result in an automatic failure of the class. Can you imagine Frank Lloyd Wright being told this? Well, after my freshman year, I could and after more research of one of the greats in architecture, I discovered he did. Well, not exactly the three-day thing, but he too was put in a box by an instructor and he later dropped out. I will never forget the instructor Mr. A telling us to *look to our left and to our right because the person you see will probably not be there with you come graduation.* I thought, *what a destroying thought, what a poor message.* All of these bright minds and that was the best he could offer. I have often reframed it this way: *look to your left and to your right and see to it that who you are looking at is with you when you graduate. See to it as a part of your success that those around you are successful as well.*

I also still had a fire in my belly that would not be extinguished, revolution. I had chosen this school, partly because of this fire in my belly. Tuskegee, with its rich history, had seen many before me with such fire. Booker T. Washington, himself, was all about change. He was teaching change in how we should view ourselves, and how we could change how the world viewed us as a race of people. Black people, being a newly emancipated people at that time, could build for themselves and change their own condition. George Washington Carver, one of the school's first professors, was revolutionizing everything from how to preserve food to assisting Henry Ford on how to revolutionize the mass manufacturing of the automobile. The school has arguably created some of the best pilots to ever take Flight, some of the best nurses to ever provide patient care, and countless activist and thought leaders. I felt the place was calling me. I quickly familiarized myself with the students whom I felt also fit the bill. When I did, I noticed a change I needed to make immediately. I had to read more. I also noticed that I needed to follow and learn from the others. So, I did just that and, in a short period, we were setting a path for change in Selma, Alabama. I remember those days, as we discussed what the issues were in Selma, and what we would do to support the high school students there who had staged a sit-in. Along with several of the other students, I traveled to Selma High School over the weekend and joined the protest. It felt like the sixties. The town still had the racist mayor, Joe Smitherman, of the 1965 march. Here it was nearly twenty five years later, and the town still had its backward system of discrimination. The black citizens were still chanting, "Joe gotta go." The town still bolstered its hatred and its terrorist group, the Ku Klux Klan, also known as the KKK. It was as if I was Michael J. Fox, and I had gone back to the future. So, it should be of no surprise that the town was still educating its black students differently than its whites. It was of no surprise that two teen members of the KKK had climbed the roof of the school to hang sheets spewing racial epithets, while the high school students lay sleeping. They had sprayed hateful remarks towards whites so it would look as if we had started the racial conflict. They were trying to get us killed. The takeover of the school made national news, and Jesse Jackson even paid us a visit. My mother and friends at home saw me on the news and were worried for my safety. I learned a lot about human behavior during that protest, and it has stayed with me since. After several years as a student activist, I was now viewed by most as a leader on campus and in the community. So, when two of my best friends to this day, Sinclair Skinner and Nik Eames, asked me to join with them to take over the financial building at Tuskegee University's Kresge Center, I was all in. I was asked to organize a field operation, getting food and other resources in for the students. Things were fine for the first night or two, but on the third day, the university, with the help of on- campus security, stopped us from getting the resources we needed. Students started getting weary, and by the following day, I requested that Sinclair allow me to organize the removal of security. With his blessing, I organized several brothers, whom I instructed to remove security. I instructed them to pick up and carry out the members of security and lock out any administrative people who left the building. That decision was the beginning of all hell breaking loose. A lot of good students were arrested and kicked out of school that day. Student government was shut down, and at the time, I regretted making that call to remove those officers. I thank God no one lost their life, because the incident had all the makings of such a thing occurring. Sinclair and Nik both got expelled and later enrolled at Howard University. A year or so later, I joined them, thanks to our brother and friend, Omar Karim. I lost touch with some of my soldiers, but I have never forgotten them. I have always felt as if I left men on the battlefield. (I had not made the best decision to have security physically removed from the building. My poor decision caused students to get expelled and some even arrested. I had not thought through my plan and had no financial means to get my men out of jail.) One major takeaway that I have learned over my many years fighting for justice is that money and power create change. If you can't hurt the pockets of those in power, then there will be no transfer of power. It was these experiences that have shaped my views on politics and the importance of controlling one's dollar. If your dollar is controlled by another, that is where you will also find your power. Being a boss is the only answer to oppression and inequality. Be a boss; be a business; be global.

Fear

"There is only one thing that makes a dream impossible to achieve: the fear of failure."
– Paulo Coelho

Some might say fear is the body's natural way to alert itself to danger. The dictionary's definition is, *"An unpleasant emotion caused by the belief that someone or something is dangerous, and likely to cause pain or threat."* For further understanding, let us explore Wikipedia's explanation of the *fight-or-flight* response (also called the fight, flight, freeze, or fawn response in post-traumatic stress disorder, hyperarousal, or the acute stress response): "It is a physiological reaction that occurs in response to a perceived harmful event, attack, or threat to survival.[1] It was first described by Walter Bradford Cannon.[a][2] His theory states that animals react to threats with a general discharge of the sympathetic nervous system, priming the animal for fighting or fleeing."

I, however, have come to the belief that fear is the mind's imagination of something misunderstood, or the lacking of knowledge of how to master a particular circumstance or situation. In short, IT'S MADE UP!

That's right; it's all a head game—one in which a well-informed and fully capable mind never perceives. I'll say it this way: danger is real, but fear is made up. If you are in the middle of the ocean and cannot swim, the danger of drowning (if you were to fall in) is real. The danger should be respected in the form of educating and preparing ourselves against the risk.

This is also true in business. Most businesses fail within the first five years. This is not because the business was necessarily a bad idea or venture, but more because of the business owner's inability to plan against risk. I'll make it plain: one should understand the business in which they involve themselves. One should educate themselves of the worst-case scenario, and have exit strategies to minimize exposure to risk. This type of planning will also minimize the danger, and allow most businesses to gain profits above and within their market of risk. So, don't practice fear; practice risk management.

Life is a pleasure, to be lived in abundance, not fear!

I was so disappointed. Here I am at the historic Tuskegee—the school that the students built brick by brick, and the school that became the largest manufacturer of bricks in the United States—and they stopped using students to design or construct the buildings on its campus. It was now in the business of lecturing, and if you missed the instructor's lecture, you might end up with an F. This was, and is, my biggest disappointment with education in this country. Education has become a big business that puts out a poor product of theorist. Many of the so called instructors have never done anything outside of academia. I touched on this earlier about a business instructor I had. He assigned each student the task of developing a business plan. (This was well after my Tuskegee University days. I was taking additional college courses at the local college and running a business.) I was excited, because I had been operating my own business for about four years. I had the obligation of staff and payroll, and had grown to be a multimillion dollar small business. So, I turned in my functioning business plan. The instructor, knowing I had a successful real estate business, would ask my advice after class. You see, his wife was trying to be a real estate investor, and he did not know how to help her, so he asked me. I was, and have always been, excited to share, so I did. Later, I discovered that my business instructor had never owned a business. He was not a business person; he just played one at colleges and universities. So, you can only imagine my frustration when I received my semester grade of a B. How could I, the teacher, get a B from his student?

Things on campus just got me angry, as buildings were being erected with no student involvement. What was this new form of education? One with a lot of talk and very little to no real application.

I had bought my first apartment building with a $203K loan. I managed bad contractors, and marketed and filled vacant units. I grew a profit and, from that profit, bought another building. Over time, I became my own contractor by paying attention to the professional carpenters, electricians, and plumbers I had hired over the years. My profit margins had grown so well, I began to hire staff. I bought building after building, and taught myself real estate finance. I got so good at rolling out the numbers, I turned abandoned buildings into cash cows. I started looking at my instructors as road blockers to my path to success. They weren't teaching me anything, but they were putting me through hell. So, to get through, I learned to give them what they wanted. While I designed my plan to success, I mastered the art of the ego stroking. Sometimes that's the politics one must play to get ahead. I noticed that, for many people, the right amount of ego boost can bring you great fortune. The best lesson here is to *allow nothing, and no one, to hinder your dreams.*

I have always been a believer in doers, not talkers, so please don't bore me with what you're going to do. Excite me with what you are doing. I am a professional trainer and public speaker, and it is easy and very fulfilling because I am talking about things that I know work. How? Because I have done them. Institutionalized education, I feel, is a game that colleges and universities play to manipulate and make huge profits, as well as give you false hope and a hell of a lot of debt. Countless people, every year, go out to pursue the college degrees. Some never finish, and many who do, graduate to a life of debt, and unfulfilling careers or jobs unrelated to their degree. I have asked the question a billion times, it seems, when attending a training where the trainer has a proven track record of success in the provided subject, and the college graduate is questioning if they should buy the course. What are you afraid of? Aren't you the one who took out a hundred thousand dollar loan in hopes of one day, after graduation, making a hundred thousand a year? This training is only two thousand, and they actually made a million dollars doing what they're teaching. It seems like a no-brainer, but today's education system doesn't teach us to think—it teaches us to take orders. Follow direction, and take a test that measures no real thing that will benefit us in today's world. The same person, who paid a hundred thousand to get the useless degree, now wants my course in real estate to pay them twenty thousand in passive income within the first week. Well, it's possible, but the real point is that getting out of your way is a total transformation.

Chapter 5

A Dream Fulfilled

"People who avoid failure also avoid success."
– Robert T. Kiyosaki

"Dreams are a visualization of one's greatness not yet manifested. The problem with those who are now realists is that they have dreams unfulfilled."
"Some of us live our dreams; others, such as realists, live their nightmare."
– Gary Rahman, *Dreamer*

My mom had years of worry and hardship. I can't even imagine, nor would I ever want to know the feeling of not being able to provide housing for my family. She begged, borrowed, and forfeited much of her pride in trying to keep us housed. I remember hearing and seeing her cry, because she couldn't make ends meet. My mom, and first true teacher, suffered from severe depression. Two parents raising three children in the big city of Chicago can have its challenges, but being single and severely depressed—well, lights out. Emily loved us, and she gave all that she knew how. I recall her pondering life, and whether this was the best she could do. Thank God she had the support of family, and a best friend, Aunt Sandra. They paid rent on many an occasion. My mom never finished high school, but she had a canny ability to inspire. As I mentioned before, she could tell a story that would have you at the edge of your seat. I think it was through this ability where she made a connection with me that I could be and do whatever I set my mind to. Here was a woman who considered suicide on more than one occasion in her life, but could channel an inner lion in me. I believed early that I could do anything; however, that didn't stop the devil from knocking, but on countless occasions, it kept him on his toes.

My mom became my biggest motivation and inspiration to do big things. I had a burning desire to prove the naysayers wrong. Being poor and uneducated was not inherent. It was important to me to legitimize my mom, and my success would do just that. Once I started making money, she no longer had to ask anyone else. I wrote the checks, but when a parent has this debilitating sickness called depression, those checks seem to be more frequent as they get older. With the help of my big sister, Sue, and my Aunt Cecilia, we were able to secure her housing at Skye 55, one of the premier condo developments on Chicago's Lakeshore Drive.

She saw me purchase and redevelop multi-unit apartment buildings, but I think she was most proud when I purchased my family home: nine bedrooms, six bathrooms, a three-car garage, and an in-ground pool. I heard her say, "You have enough rooms now that none of us would ever be outdoors". So, to have her here to see the birth of her first grandchild being born, with a silver spoon in his mouth, was truly a dream fulfilled.

With a newborn son and a growing business, life was good; and it seemed like it would only get better. With a son, I was now motivated because I now had someone to leave the empire I was building. Callie and I had done our estate planning several years before Kali was born. We had our Trust drafted with the utmost detail. Our children would receive a non-interest loan from the trust for education. They would receive certain amounts annually, based upon the level of education they earned. They would have to take finance courses and learn money management prior to any allotment. They would receive bonus allotments for a first marriage, birth of children, and, of course, the purchase of a home. All allotments would have an ending point in order to allow the children's natural desires to develop. So, the birth of Kali was the beginning of a legacy.

Shortly after his birth, I had won a HUD auction that was going to allow me to build a hundred-unit building from the ground up. (HUD stands for Department of Housing and Urban Development) It was a base build construction project, which had been another goal of mine. I was building my team of architects, finance *cats*, and real estate attorneys for this very moment. Now, I was going to get my break to turn the real corner of wealth. I will share the number by percentages to maintain this book's power for further generation and inflation. I was already a millionaire, both with liquid and tangible assets. My monthly passive income was in the top one percent of the country's earners. Once this deal was completed, I would more than double my monthly passive income, and my annual income would be among the top one percent of the one percent. To make it plain, I would be amongst the richest people in the country, grossing nearly 2 million a year in passive income. This is the kid who was in a learning disability class, had a mother on welfare, and a daddy absent from his life—on the verge of making a passive income of 2 million a year. But I never sold drugs, or robbed anyone to get here. But when things got better for me, life still had to provide more education and more lessons, so that I would never return to poverty. It did not seem that I was ready. Some city officials in Baltimore didn't like the fact I had beat them in the auction. Many, I think, also didn't like my plans to build affordable housing for the elderly. I noticed that, in many cities, towns, and states, Poverty is big business. Keeping the disenfranchised uneducated, unhoused, and legally unrepresented is the way many in government and business want it. So, when I beat out the city, they sent attack dogs from every angle. The word on the street was, "WHO IS THIS DC BOY BUYING BUILDINGS HERE IN BALTIMORE?" When I got word of this from my friend on the inside, I was pissed. Hell, I'm not from DC; I'm from Chicago. I was told that people in the mayor's office, and in housing, didn't like that I had won, and didn't care what I was planning to do on the site. They didn't care that I was planning on building affordable housing for our seniors, even though the city was being fined for not having enough affordable housing. All they wanted was to destroy this deal for me and regain the control of the land. Knowing this, I pressed forward. I was working 20-hour days. I couldn't sleep, and my typical day went something like this: up by 6:00 am; out by 7:30 am; to be in the mayor's office or some financial person's office by 8:00 am, and no later than 9:00 am, I would have meetings until about 7:00 pm with contractors and other team members, returning home by 8:00 pm, working on the numbers and making calls in my home office until about 2:00 am; sleeping for four hours, and then repeating the process the next day. I did this for weeks with a newborn baby at home, and a wife who wanted me to help out more during late night feedings. The city told HUD that I was not planning on adhering to the contract detail of razing the current structure. Where the city got this information was news to me. I had all the intentions of following the contract but, because of a lie, I had to hire attorneys to provide me a press release. That still didn't stop the madness: I was now hopping from one meeting with the mayor's offices to one with housing. HUD then changed the term of the agreement, like a true gangster. I now I had to come up with a letter of credit, with only two days to do it in. I worked every angle I knew how. I got an extension by using my phone records to prove HUD wrong on what was agreed upon.

But it wasn't enough time, and they took my hundred thousand dollar earnest deposit, and a multi-million dollar deal, right out of my hands. They later tried to re-auction the property, and my inexperienced attorney got a stay order. They offered me the deal back in court at a time that the banks were no longer lending due to the crash of the real estate market. I sued HUD, only to find out later that my attorney filed the case in the wrong jurisdiction to go forward. After thousands of dollars in legal fees, I was done, and the powers that live off the poverty of the poor had won the battle, but I wanted more fuel to win the war. I got schooled, and I learned more than any college professor could have ever taught me.

Why I would do it again

I not only believe, but I know, the most successful people are doers. They make decisions quickly and solve problems that others have no answer for. I know some deals didn't go as planned, but what I learned could not be taught in a class. Falling on my face in 2008 was perhaps one of the greatest business lessons of my career. It forced me to study, to read, and to be more humble. Every time we fall, we should learn. Every time we succeed, we should be humble and whether we are winning or losing, we should always be reading. These challenges have strengthened me and as

I build my brand, I do it knowing I'm stronger and wiser than before. My message is more compelling and my answers are more precise. I've illuminated my weak areas, and work on them daily. If you think you know it all, you haven't failed big enough yet. But it's coming and the bigger you are when it does come, more devastating it will be. Get in the lab fast; study, read and seek knowledge from those more successful than you. Ask questions and be ok being the dummy in the room. There are a lot of dumb billionaires that were smart enough to be dumb at the right time. Let that be you.

Living a winning life

Living a winning life is about more than the end result. Anyone making money or doing things that only money can buy will often be looked at as a winner. The true meaning for me is more about the process or the journey than the end result.

Ask any great athlete what is the highest point or zone like state and when is it most apparent and they will all agree that it is not at the final buzzer. Living a winning life is more about challenging your perceived limitations and transcending them in order to expand and vibrate on a higher frequency. That higher frequency is like a euphoric state and when we arc closest to our Creator. So many fail to ever know this feeling, because they dare to live. I say challenge everything. My marriage is great not because we never have issues, but because we challenge each other to expand. We allow each other the freedom to search ourselves and the space to grow. In business I have made millions of mistakes, but I have enjoyed the growth. I have learned to be patient with myself and allow the lessons to soak in and nurture my roots. Living a winning life is not worrying about if you have the right answer, it's about being ok that you don't and just asking for it. It is the fun, it's the uncertainty about the seconds ahead and the confidence knowing that eventually you'll be on top. If you're not feeling this way about your life then you're not living. If you're not living, you're certainly not winning.

Chapter 6

Devil Makes a Comeback

"What would you do if you knew the date of your death? Would you tell your spouse how beautiful they are and enjoy each intimate moment, connecting with them on a deeper level, or spend your time wondering who they would be with once you're gone? Would you pay more attention to your children, and truly see them as the gifts they are to the world, or would you tell them what to be and how to live, simply to fit in?"
– Gary Rahman, Death Wish

"Beginning today, treat everyone you meet as if they were going to be dead by midnight. Extend to them all the care, kindness, and understanding you can muster, and do it with no thought of any reward. Your life will never be the same again."
– Og Mandino

You've heard the saying, "It was the best of times; it was the worst of times." Well, I know exactly what that means. My wife, Callie, and I tried for four years to have children before the Creator blessed us with the miracle of our son, Kali. So, we were ecstatic as we waited for the arrival of our daughter, Spirit. My business was going through its toughest year ever. I had to let my staff go, and my credit was in the toilet. I had several buildings underwater and many pending foreclosure. It was so bad, I went to work for one of my best friends, and it all felt like hell. I was deeply depressed and drinking heavily. The devil had his hand around my neck, and I wanted him to slit my throat.

Just two years prior, I had a net worth of seven million dollars, and a million of that was cash. I was grossing over four hundred thousand a year in rental income, and working on this biggest deal of my career. I was developing a hundred-unit apartment building that was going to be grossing me over 90 grand a month. I was planning on my life sky rocketing to the moon, but instead, because of a local politician and the Department of Housing and Urban Development, my business was imploding. They had changed the terms just days before the closing, not allowing me the necessary time to secure the additional funding. It was unbelievable that a council member of a poor community, and a government agency whose mission is to assist in the development of housing for the poor, was destroying a small business whose mission is to provide housing for the poor in underserved communities. I was losing my mind; the devil was beating me, but I had a secret weapon. Her name was Emily, and she believed I was a rainmaker. So I was also looking forward to her visit after the birth of my daughter because I needed a shot of *mama love*. The delivery date for Spirit had arrived, and my mind was occupied with her birth. It was one of the happiest moments of my life. She was healthy and beautiful and full of life. The announcement of her birth was made, and my mom celebrated with friends. Callie and I spent the first two days in the hospital, and I needed to finish a few daddy duties at home. So, I along with my brother, who was in town for Spirit's birth, left to get some work done. Only hours after we left did I get one of the worst calls of my life. Emily, our mom had a massive heart attack and had been resuscitated twice. She was now in critical condition. The news felt like a bomb had exploded in my head, and the devil seemed to be playing a game with my heart. I was on the last *thing burning* to Chicago from

Baltimore. I arrived at the hospital to be greeted by my sister and two of my best friends, Phil Burton and Kendall Jones. I will never forget them for being there; it meant the world to me. I had made it just in time to see my mother's eyes open for the last time of her life. So, here I was, the last 48 hours had taken me to the highest of highs, and now to the lowest of lows. The devil had made a comeback, and I was down for the count. Trying my best to understand all of this was taxing. Just days ago, I was so happy to be waiting for the arrival of my daughter, and it was a timely lift because my business was hurting. I was still making a large monthly amount, but debt had increased due to the market crash, and many of my interest payments had doubled, or even tripled, and I was bleeding through savings, trying to make payroll for the last couple of employees that still remained. It was so bad, I was working for a friend as his assistant and property manager, and it was the hardest job I had ever had—largely because my friend was an ass to work for. I would work a twelve or fifteen-hour day, and he would complain that I didn't finish an assignment. We had gotten into a heated conversation, and he, in so many words, called me a thief. He later was proven incorrect, and discovered that he actually owed me money. I continued to work for him, but I didn't view him the same after that. He was out of town when all hell was breaking loose for me personally, but I continued to manage his affairs while in Chicago at my mom's bedside. I was a man of my word, whether he knew it or not. I returned after my mother's passing and he treated me as if I had been enjoying the beach. I was expected to pick right back up as if I hadn't experienced my greatest loss to date. I didn't say much afterwards, but I continued to work hard. I had once told him I would clean shit for my family, and I really felt he wanted me to prove it. I worked as if his business was mine, but with no appreciation from him. I did it until one month to the day of my mother's passing, when he suspended me for failing an inspection. I was so angry, all I could do was cry to keep myself from killing him. I told him I was done, and I would return all the keys to his 150 plus units and growing real estate holdings. I loved this guy so much; we had shared and supported each other over the years prior while our businesses were growing. I expected more from him during this hard time, and it hurt so badly. I knew that I had to get back on my feet, so I looked inward. I didn't harbor any bad feelings with my friend, which I think surprised him. A year or two later, he apologized and gave me a gift that was life changing: a first edition copy of Napoleon Hill's *Laws of Success.* I began to slowly put the pieces back together and to reflect on where I had come from. My friend, would some years later assisted me in having my largest grossing year to date of 2.1 million. Forgiveness is freeing and helps us make room for growth. So, take a lesson from me, because holding onto anger can costs more than it's worth.

Depression

I felt like I had a gorilla standing on my chest. My thoughts were jumbled, my focus was off, and death seemed to overwhelm me. Is this how my mother felt? Depression is a real sickness. Many have gone through small episodes, but some live a life of chronic depression. Like my mother and my brother. For most of my life I believed that those suffering from the disease were making excuses. They just didn't want to work; they were lazy. My wife is a clinically licensed social worker, and she had been educating me about how the disease is not one that can be controlled by will or desire. I was now understanding this in real time. I had always been a self-starter. With will and desire to match, I dared not allow what I thought to be a fake sickness take me out, but it almost did. I wanted to touch on this disease for several reasons. First, because I hope to foster empathy for those stricken with this chemical imbalance. A disease that affects millions every year, many who kill themselves because of the lack of the medical attention needed to manage the disease. Some live with the stigma that the sickness is either not real or that they're crazy. One might think that someone like me, with a mother and brother that suffered or continues to battle the disease, would understand it better. But for a long time I didn't. Depression can be the devil's secret weapon. It can destroy dreams and kill futures, both figuratively and literally speaking. Yet there is hope. I fortunately was only dealing with a small episode due to my mom's sudden death and the real estate market in the tank, but many of my readers may suffer from the actual disease. I urge you not to let this take you off course or distract you from your dreams. Diet and medication have both proven to help people live productive lives. Remember when you have a *Why* that is big enough, no sickness or ailment will cause you to lose.

How to get to tomorrow

I used to believe that tomorrow would never come. When you're a child, days seem like years and years seem like lifetimes. But in reality, we know life is not this way at all. But trying to convince someone in the pits of hell that tomorrow will be a better day can be a feat as big as climbing Everest. I'm speaking to you from experience of being a poor kid, born to a mother who didn't finish high school, and father who wanted her to abort me. I'm telling you from my memories of missed meals and hunger pains. I'm telling you from my memories of a child stressed by adult concerns of eviction and homelessness. Being poor in a rich nation is both emotionally and physically taxing. So how do you get to tomorrow? The short answer is simple, and you've heard it before. One day at a time. I didn't for a long time understand or believe this to be true, or to bring any value. Today, however, I understand it simply to mean stay present. So often we get so fixated on our current situation that we fail to put any thought towards the solutions for what we need to fix. Staying present in life does two major things. It helps us to appreciate how far we've traveled, and lets us focus on what we must do next to get through that moment. Look, tomorrow is not promised to any of us, so worrying about it causes unnecessary stress and no solutions for today's problem. The fact is if you don't work on not drowning right now, the shark you may encounter won't matter. I have become like a Zen master with an understanding that problems are created to exercise our mind and our will. Take the stress off and write a plan. Revise that plan as often as necessary. It will help you stay present as you work only on what is before you at the time. The universe will do the rest in the order in which you need them and on a perfect schedule. So, just work your ass off today, right now, at this very moment, and if you're blessed enough to see tomorrow, it will again honor you with a present. Don't throw today away for what may never come, tomorrow.

Follow greatness

I believe in reading, but once in my life this was a major challenge. So I'm not sure if that's why I love to read, but it has truly helped me in difficult moments in my life. Reading someone else's story, their ups and downs throughout life, is fascinating to me. It's like having a special pair of glasses that allows me to see what works and what doesn't. With all the information available to us today, we can build wealth or success faster and better than previous generations. People like Reginald Lewis, Og Mandingo, and of course Napoleon Hill have inspired and motivated me with their stories. I'm also a student of some amazing people today. On Twitter I follow Richard Branson, Oprah Winfrey, Warren Buffett, Sean Puffy Combs a.k.a. Diddy, and some of the greatest and brightest minds in business today. I love Damon Dash. His understanding of entrepreneurship and the responsibilities of being a boss is refreshing and honest. But my own circle of influence is pretty impressive and consists of tomorrow's big name influencers. Sinclair Skinner, Jerome Bailey, Dr. Maya Rockeymoore Cummings, Marilyn Mosby, King Raj Singh, Demetrius Felder, Gena Lofton, Robert Raymond Riopel, Enoch Muhammad, Omar Karim and Katerina Cozias to name a few. The only point here is to follow greatness, because there is no secret why the great ones all knew each other before the world knew them.

Stay connected

Staying connected is not a cliché but a statement of a transformative nature. I like to stay connected to the community and everyday people. They seem to charge my Spirit with energy to go to work. I love meeting people and hearing their stories. It's fascinating what people have experienced, and how they survived some of life's challenges. It is ironic, however, how most don't see themselves as winning. Almost two years ago I started my radio show Connection where I interview people from all over the world. The premise of the show is that the guest shares their stories and we come up with solutions to build better communities connecting the dots of wealth, health, and education through Real Estate. It is right up my alley having a social political format that is solution driven. I never imagined myself doing radio before, but now I can't imagine not doing radio. Hearing the stories of so many amazing people, and their triumphs in life, has been mind blowing, but this connection has also fed my soul. It has inspired and motivated me to fight another day towards my why. The human connection is God's gift to us. It allows us to see our greatness in others so that we can also manifest our gifts to others. Staying connected helps us to understand what we desire physically, mentally, and emotionally through experience of others.

Fool's gold is everywhere

It's so pretty, especially when you catch it in the right light. I've been fixated myself by its charm. I have felt the blood rush through me due to excitement of the thought of what was next, with my mouth watering, my heart beating, about to explode, and being mesmerized by such a thing of beauty. But it wasn't just me that was under its hypnotic spell. I have in my lifetime seen countless people chase it. Families destroyed over it. Nations have started wars to get their hands on as much as possible. Lives have been ended because of what they believed it to be

.

That's how it gets you. Fool's gold. (Brassy yellow mineral, especially pyrite, that can be mistaken for gold.) It's everywhere when you have no direction. Life is funny like that. It will place at your feet all the vices in the world. From beautiful women, men, money, drugs, and for many the most irresistible of them all, sex. It knows when and how to approach. It's seductive, cunning and charismatic. It's got preachers, priests and politicians as some of its favorite victims, but it's also got teachers, daddies, and mothers too. All of us have played the fool one time or another. I believe two reasons for this are because of the following. One fool's gold is everywhere. You can't escape it. The other more reflective reason is that our why in life is not big enough. I can't say this enough. If you don't focus on a purpose, a goal with some depth and meaning, you will chase after things with glitter but no substance. You will measure yourself by material possessions rather than worldly impact. Drifting is the biggest enemy of time. What occupies your mind is the thing that gets your attention. Where you have placed your time is what you have valued as your gold. So what you really want, you have. If you have nothing, you have spent your time doing nothing. If you have money, that's where your time has been spent. Feeling overly sexed? Check your time. Friends got you down? How much time have placed in their care? Eliminating the noise out of your life is your true salvation, and the yellow brick road to Oz. Fool's gold is everywhere, so if you're going to be successful know your Why.

Remember your team works for you

In real estate and really in any business, you need a great team to grow a great business. In the space of real estate, that consists of attorneys, accountants, contractors, lenders, insurance agents, and sometimes real estate agents and sometimes property managers.

Some people, when embarking on this business, wait until they have all their members in place before doing their first deal. Others jump in and build members as they go. I did it somewhere in the middle. I got key members like my agents and lender in place early, and I've continued to change members as I grow. The truth is that many don't understand my business and just play the role they were taught. Well, if you're going to grow and become a large successful business, you want team members that get it. They have to want to be as big as you. It's been my experience that if your team members want to be great they will be more creative when advising you. In the beginning, and sometimes even now, I have felt like I was in the twilight zone. I can recall explaining what I wanted from one of my team members and them giving me another result. Some have even gotten sensitive when I've needed to correct them on their falling short of the desired outcome. Look, I believe in being loyal and treating everyone with respect, but don't confuse being respectful with acceptance of incompetence or a team member that continues to underperform. This is business; it not personal. If you can't differentiate this I would also advise you never to hire family or friends. I have no issue firing those that don't meet my expectations, but it hasn't always been this way. I have seen some of the most successful do this early on and consistently. It makes no sense or cents to pay someone who doesn't perform as agreed.

The Matrix is a mother

If you've ever seen the movie the Matrix than you can't forget the scene when Morpheus gives Neo the option. "You take the **blue pill**, the story ends. ... You take the **red pill**, you stay in Wonderland, and I show you how deep the rabbit hole goes." Well, if you haven't tapped out yet, I guess you're here for the full trip? This trip is a **Mother!** of pawns fighting and dying over crap never even intended for them. So once you understand this maybe you will start to play the game differently. At least that's my hope. It took me years of taking crap to learn all that I have learned. My skin has been thickened. I am not saying I'm the "one" but I am saying that after four hundred years of oppression and delusion of poor whites. The Matrix's powers have slowed, or perhaps I've quickened. Either way, understand now that what most people want or consider success is indeed that of Alice in Wonderland, a never-ending rabbit hole. I want to teach you to play smarter, full on with a purpose to transform lives. The age of materialism, sexism and racism must come to an end to grow into our true greatness. A greatness that is not measured by dollar signs but by how much you can impact the world. Truth is, it's always been about transformation but the Matrix is a mother that will have poor people of different colors fight against each other over shades of gray, while government and colonialism elites continue to push the carrot further out of reach for both black and white poor. I feel called to share and put folks on *game*. So, I guess you know I took the red pill and I'm oh so glad I did.

It's worth it if it's your purpose

I was hungry, living on friends' dorm room floors or alternating between this friend's and that friend's housed. I ate peanut butter and jelly mainly, but sometimes a friend would flip me their meal card and I would visit the Blackburn Cafe. I sold Kirby vacuum cleaners at $1500.00 a pop. It was a hundred percent commission based opportunity, and I quickly learned the principal *you eat what you kill*. I found myself in Washington DC, and I refused to ever go back to Chicago to live until I could buy a lakefront condo on Chicago's magnificent mile. My story's humble beginning is familiar to so many success stories I've either read or heard. One of my favorite movies of all time is *Baadasssss!,* the story of Melvin Van Peebles making of the highest grossing independent films of its time. Van Peebles lost the sight in one eye because of the stress of making the historic *Sweet Sweetback*. There are countless stories like this, but one thing is always consistent among the successful. Nothing else seems to matter, and no tear is too big to drown in. If you want it, go get it, if it has purpose.

She Brought Me Out

"Be strong, believe in freedom and in God, love yourself, understand your sexuality, have a sense of humor, masturbate, don't judge people by their religion, color or sexual habits, love life and family."
– Madonna

"Today, I woke up with a brand new optimism on life. So, I am not concerned with what happened yesterday. It is buried with all the disappointment and with all its glory. Today's opportunities are the best I have ever had. It's even better than tomorrow because only today matters. Only what I do today can change how my tomorrow will be birthed."
Gary Rahman, *Today*

I never saw her in this way before. Sure, she was beautiful and loving, but now she represented more for me. Prior to my mom's death, we were having our own personal issues, and it seemed that each moment was more fragile than the next. I wanted and needed her to step up and take on a bigger role in our household. My beautiful wife, Callie, was truly the deepest romantic love of my life, but now she was draining me. It seemed that everything she did annoyed me. But the day she announced one of my deal breakers, at a family celebration, I felt I was done. Christmas was on the table, and I felt betrayed and even lied to. All I could think was, *how could she?* We had discussed this prior to marriage, and had agreed that the fat, jolly man and his holiday would not be celebrated in our family. I know, for some of my readers, this may cause you to checkout; but historically, the holiday has nothing to do with the birth of Jesus. It's as pagan a holiday as they come, but that's for another book. For this one, Callie and I had agreed: no Christmas. We were raising two beautiful children, and the outside pressure from both of our families to give the children gifts was too much. She now wanted to celebrate Christmas which for me was a deal breaker. She shared how tense the house was with family and friends. I even discussed with two of my best friends, David Kenney and Larry Bobo, my idea of a separation. I thank God for them both; at a time during great vulnerability, they both talked me off that ledge. I love black people so much, and the destruction of black families only further erodes our communities. But even with this knowledge and desire not to continue a destructive cycle, we were not out of the woods yet. I was hurting, I hadn't really recovered from the blows I had taken from my failing business. I was still very sad and lonely from the loss of my mom, and I wasn't sure Callie could be what I needed. Our sex life was suffering, and I felt very little connection, but I loved her, and as badly as things seemed, I knew she loved me too.

I started to notice something huge. I noticed as I surrendered and allowed her to care for my wounds— she was healing me. I opened up and told her what I needed, and she listened with ears keen to my voice and with a heart to comfort my soul. When we made love, we made it with deep connection, both with a desire to truly provide the other with the protection and strength to conquer whatever we faced together. I was seeing and understanding that she was, and is, my best friend. Times were still unstable financially, but now it seemed temporary. I still missed and longed for my mom, but now I felt a new sense of comfort and assurance. The Rahmans were going to be fine, and it was all because of this amazing woman who I had overlooked and underestimated.

The devil had me in his den, but Callie brought me out. But how could I have forgotten? It may very well have been the best day of my life—if not, it surely was one of them. I woke up that morning, as I recall, with an attitude of thankfulness. I loved this season of the year, as the trees brown and the nights begin to cool. At the

Hyatt Hotel, where I was a young hotel manager, we were hosting one of my favorite conferences. It was Congressional Black Caucus Foundation week, also known as CBCF. Prior to the CBCF week, I had only experienced my fraternity's conclave, which boasted of such highly educated and well-rounded black professionals. The energy was electric, and the people were beautiful. So, imagine my pleasure when one of the major sponsors of the event, the late great Benjamin S. Ruffin, Vice President of Corporate Affairs at R. J. Reynolds, personally invited me to be a guest at his table for their signature formal Phoenix dinner. The Phoenix dinner guests were all the black members of congress, and some of the most powerful and accomplished people in the world. So, to share in my experience, I invited a couple of close friends: Arnold Bryant, and his girlfriend, Towanda (*now Mr. And Mrs. Bryant*). We stepped out that evening looking like new money, and we were enjoying the night so much that, after the dinner, we decided to go back to the hotel for a night cap—which would turn out to be one of the best decisions of my life. In Arnold's quest to secure parking upon our arrival to the hotel, it happened: that moment or experience when one is faced with love at first sight. I had never believed that such a thing could happen, but here I was, with my heart beating faster than ever as this beautiful young lady and her friend crossed our path to her car. Arnold stopped to get her parking spot, and I immediately jumped out to introduce myself. I felt confident in my tux, for tonight had been a rebirthing, and I could not lose. So, as I introduced myself, she reciprocated with *Callie*. She seemed polite and open to my advancement but did not give me her number as I requested to perhaps reconnect. Although disappointed, I did not feel defeated. I bid both her and her friend a goodnight as I began my walk back to the company of my friends. Once again, the Universe did its thing, and forced her friend, who I had obviously impressed, to blow the car horn, insisting that Callie call me back. Again at her car door, Callie requested my number, and I was happy to fulfill her request. It would be two weeks before I heard from her, but during our first conversation, it was as if we had known each other for years. We talked for hours about everything and nothing. I looked forward to our many talks because it turned out that three months had passed before we were able to connect for a date. You see, I lived in Washington DC, and Callie had only been visiting from Philadelphia the night we met, during CBCF week.

Callie suggested a date to the Blacks in Wax Museum in Baltimore. The date spoke to my soul, and Callie was both beautiful and refreshing. By our third date, which was just a few weeks after our first, I knew it. I knew that I had met my future wife, and my stomach was bursting with butterflies (a feeling that astonished me for I had been somewhat of a Casanova). I told my mother and my friends the news, and from knowing me with the ladies, they were shocked, yet excited to witness our courtship. Callie was pushing all the right buttons. She was affectionate and caring, yet she offered the right amount of space so as not to suffocate, allowing the perfect mix to foster a longing for more of her affection. She was a good listener. It was evident as she suggested we have a budget for what had become our by-monthly visits to each of our respective cities. This suggestion was like music to my ears. I was planning on buying my first apartment building and watching my spending was a must. Life was good, and only got better when she also took on the challenge of buying a building too. My family and friends, after three years, now understood my sentiment after only our third date. She was beautiful to the eyes but even more so to the spirit. Her laugh could fill a room, and it made me feel as if God was present. I was in heaven; the devil was dead; and life could only get better—and that it did. So, on her 31st birthday, I wanted to ensure that she knew how I felt about her. I asked her Dad for his blessing; and I asked her mom, her cousin, Daniella, and her best friend, Renata, who was with her the night we'd met, to help me in picking out the ring. Again, this was one of the best decisions. These three women have been so supportive in our union, and I love them all arguably as much as Callie does. Well, maybe not that much, but my affection for each of them is large. So, not only was I being blessed to marry a beautiful woman, I got another mother and two more sisters, and I would be remiss if I didn't acknowledge the abundant blessing of having a father. Daddy Jack, was, and is, the icing on my cake. He truly is the father I wished for. He and I debate and challenge each other, but mainly love and respect each other. I knew that the Creator had blessed me beyond measure, and I was excited to ask Callie to be my wife.

Being the planner I am, I scheduled a trip to Nassau, Bahamas. I told Callie it would be to celebrate her birthday. We had gone on trips before and, because of my status in the hotel business, it was always five star treatment, which we both enjoyed. In planning, I mailed to the Bahamas, in advance, a dress, shoes, and make-up for her to don on the special day of my proposal, so as not to tip her off by suggesting she bring such things. It was amazing as I finalized all the details with the hotel, from where I would pop the question, to how I would document the occasion with pictures, and have singers to build the moment. I wanted all to be perfect for her, because she was truly the love of my life. The night was everything, and more, as we shared smiles, tears, and a planned beachfront dinner for two. I was the happiest man alive, and would have married her that night, had we not had wishes of sharing the moment with family and friends. We planned for a year and a half, considering all the smallest of details. Each person we asked to honor us in being a part of our special day was selected with deep reflection on our lives. Each guest was meaningful, and we wanted to honor them all. The ceremony was an outdoor event overlooking the Chesapeake Bay, at the beautiful Officer's Club, on the Aberdeen Proving Grounds. We had 300 guests from all over the country and one from Japan. The energy was loving and unforgettable, and though it rained during the ceremony, it was filled only with sunshine. In honor of our guests, we donated ten dollars in the name of each of them to the Tom Joyner Foundation, which provides scholarships to students who attend historically black colleges and universities. It was the start of a great life: I was rich; I had the woman of my dreams; our mission in life as a couple was clear; and we were honeymooning in Africa for nearly a month. Like all things, the honeymoon must end. When it did, I had to reevaluate what she meant to me. But how could I have forgotten?

Chapter 7

Devil on the Run

"I will live this day as if it is my last. And if it is not, I shall fall to my knees and give thanks."
– Og Mandino

I was a man possessed. I was reading everything, and traveling the country to hear from the top industry leaders in marketing, sales, business, and self-improvement. I had always dreamed big, but I was now on a stage where dreaming big was the special of the day. I joined the number one, self-improvement organization in the world: New Peaks. New Peaks, which is now Success Resources of America, connected me with some of the most thought-provoking people I have ever met. This organization was connected with greats like Tony Robbins, the billion dollar man, Berny Dohrmann, T. Harv Eker, Joel Roberts, Jeff Hoffman, Raymond Aaron, JT Foxx, Ken Courtright, and a list that goes on and on. I was pushed to think bigger, to plan better, and to give more, and love harder. It was great, and I was sold. I realized that the world, which I loved so dearly, needed me, and New Peaks was showing me how to serve them. I always loved a true teacher: you know, the ones with the battle scars, with a story, each one more amazing and compelling than the last. This place was loaded with *doers*. I had found a home where I was being coached and mentored by the best. Ken Courtwright and I made such a real connection, that I must thank him now. His openness to share has given me a voice today that demands to be heard. He told me never to give another business card out without first sharing my story. He also told me to be careful who I choose as a mentor because, if my dreams were bigger than theirs, they may try to sabotage me unknowingly. I reflect often on both of those discussions, and a host of others, which he has shared with me over the last few years. New Peaks has many trainers, but one in particular has been huge in my life over the last four years: Robert Raymond Riopel. The amazing thing is, of all the many courses I have taken with New Peaks, the Universe only provided this one trainer for me. Some would question why, but I have not; he has meant more than words can express. He has not only been a trainer; he has been a friend. With all these incredible mentors and coaches, I have been able to get my inside game right—that mindset needed for a rough battleground. I was ready to take on the devil again; but this time, he didn't have a shot. I was armed with a beautiful wife, two great children, and a community of overachievers, teaching me how to conquer all. But mainly, what I had rediscovered was the burning desire of that ten-year-old boy who wanted to serve the world. I now had my *why* back, and the devil was once again on the run.

I know, many people find it hard to believe that mindset is the true key to success. So many feel it has something to do with luck and preparation. I believe there is nothing lucky about being prepared. And besides, being prepared is only a small part of success. The larger, and more important part, is your will. A strong will has a way of defeating the best and most noted talent. I have never been the smartest in my circle. As I mentioned, I was the runt of the litter, academically, amongst my friends. I wasn't the most connected either, but one thing that has assured me a real opportunity, has been my attitude. I, for the most part, have had an attitude of *no surrender, no defeat.* I find no excuses for my shortcomings, other than to correct them, and that I do. It has been a goal of mine to become a great writer, so I read great writings, and I write often. I made a goal to be a billionaire real estate investor developer by 2030, and the Universe introduced me to people like Berny Dohrmann, of CEO Space, and Jeff Hoffman, founder of Priceline.com. Berny has shown me the holes in my armor, and charged me with improving and connecting my purpose to my people. Berny Dohrmann: the godson of Napoleon Hill, and even more impressive, the billion dollar man, who went to jail for securities fraud but has built himself back up as a leader in business. Berny has the scars and the wounds of a true teacher, and I appreciate him for sharing his mistakes and how I can be better.

No matter what the devil has thrown my way, it has not dimmed my light, nor has it weakened my will. I knocked him down, and it felt like child's play. Each day, I become more focused and more driven to attain my *why*. My mindset is clear, and those around me are like-minded, or they no longer remain in my space. This is sacred ground, and I'm doing God's work. So, yes, I will not be denied—the Universe will give me all that I want. This is not hocus-pocus; this is universal law.

If you have a dream, put yourself in an environment that can foster that dream. Be around people who understand and believe in this law. If you spend most of your time with dream killers, universal law will eventually kill your dream and desire. It is better to be alone than to be among dream killers. I can't stress this enough, but I will reframe it this way: ask and seek out people doing what you want to do in life; read what they read; listen to what they listen to; travel to the places they travel to; and learn what they offer to teach. The devil's tricks are nothing but child's play.

Other believers

Stop telling and start doing. Yes, there is a time to call things into existence, but always remember that actions speak louder than words. Do you recall my story about my college business professor? Well, if you do you already know how I feel about anyone who doesn't have skin in the game. So much is going on around the world and it seems like almost everyone is complaining about something. It's quite perplexing how they don't seem to search for their own solutions. They just keep complaining and pointing fingers. I often think about what a waste of all this brain power. The human brain has enough energy to light a lightbulb or charge a cell phone. Doing is the only answer. I don't have to make you a believer. I can and will prove to you that what I plan is real by doing it. I know I'm making it sound quite simple but the phenomenal thing is that it is. I was ten years old and couldn't read, and said I would be a millionaire. Steve Jobs created something called the Internet. The Egyptians built the pyramids by using solar and lunar light and understanding shadow. So, the simplest way to create believers and breathe life into their ideas is by showing them how you manifest yours. As we evolved as a species, we have become smarter, faster, and more innovative because our survival and consciousness forces us to. So, if you're not already, it is time that you became a believer in you.

When it makes sense

When it make sense there is probably a reason. I really don't care what others think of me or what they are saying about me. I am my own man, and I think for myself. Don't get me wrong, I love all people, and as I've already said, I believe the human connection to be God's true gift. That, however, doesn't mean I follow your path as if it is mine.

\

So, think for yourself in life but especially as it applies to business. I can't count the many times I was either given the incorrect answer or I was told no from someone who could not give me a yes in the first place. They had either no knowledge of what I asked or no authority to grant my request. Get the right answer. We are surrounded by people with self doubt, resentment, and super egos.

Chapter 8

Manifest Greatness

"Recognize that life is a cruel taskmaster, and that either you master it or it masters you. There is no halfway or compromising point. Never accept from life anything you do not want. If that which you do not want is temporarily forced upon you, you can refuse, in your mind, to accept it, and it will make way for the thing you do want."
– Napoleon Hill, *Outwitting the Devil*

I do my best work at night when others are sleeping and dreaming of a *better* life. I like to be working on making the *best* one. The nights are quiet and provide an opportunity to think clearly. So, learn to take a moment to be still and think. This may sound strange, but the truth is that most people are not thinkers. Many just follow the crowd and have never really trained themselves to be thinkers. This is a pivotable thing to learn if you are planning on being successful at anything. Why? Because the noise of the world can cloud or silence our inner voice. When I'm in my thinking, creative zone, in my creative space, which is in my office, I don't like music or television playing. I want to be free of outside distractions when I am tapping into my genius. Yes, my *genius*. We all have it: you're born both a winner and a genius. Most just fail to recognize these gifts, because the devil has a million and one distractions. How can you expect to be your best *you* if you're not willing to avoid the distraction? We have to stay focused, and stop the drifting long enough to accomplish what we want. One of the first things I tell everyone to do is to write your goals.

Writing down things I want has some type of subconscious effect. Writing down my goal surely helps me in getting focused and providing direction. Without direction, how does one know where to start? So, pick something and write it down. It will also prove my commitment for the goal, assisting me with my motivation. Motivation feeds the desire, which for me is a main ingredient. Desire kills the noise from the naysayers, but it also filters out the biggest killer of my dreams—the devil within. More dreams are killed by the dream maker than by anyone else, and writing my goals down is my defense against myself. Writing down my goals is also a means of checks and balances. It helps me keep score or measure myself. If I, or you, intend on achieving a certain thing, measuring ourselves is essential to our success. That which is between our ears is not just matter. It can be what gets us through those difficult times, or what takes us out. So, a written goal is a starting point of future success.

Next, is speaking what I want into existence. I'm not talking witchcraft. I'm talking about being so firm in what I want that telling others only helps me attract more of what I need from the Universe. So, speak it, and speak it often. I have the opportunity to speak it to thousands of people, every week, on my radio show, Connection, but even telling your inner circle can make you more grounded.

In my friend, David Corbin's book, *Illuminate: Harnessing the Positive Power of Negative Thinking*, he speaks to another important point and practice. He makes us look at what's not working, identify what's broken, and shed light on it. It's affirmation for me to measure myself. It also helps me to eliminate people who may be draining me, or are just not a good fit. See, becoming successful is not just an idea; it is an overall transformation. It will not be fooled by catchy tricks or inconsistent effort. It takes vision, work, will, and strong mental presence. I've been faced with death, bankruptcy, lawsuits, foreclosures, and a host of other worldly challenges. Having a road map of what I want has continuously got me through some of my darkest days. I share these challenges so that you understand that they are not foreign to me, nor will they be to you. You may have even faced some of them already, but having a written set of goals can keep you focused, no matter what.

Check your circle of influence. Well, you might think you don't have a circle of influence. Sounds important, doesn't it? That's because it is, and whether you know you have one or not, you do. However, it may not be helping you reach your goals. In fact, it may be helping you to sabotage them. You may have heard it before: your success is in direct proportion to the five people you spend the most time with. This is sadistically true; so, as I said before, who are the people in your life that are not a good fit with where you want to be? It may be time to purge. I know this sound harsh to some, but if I'm doing God's work, then my *why* makes this essential. Cut the dead weight, and stop doing *general population shit*. My friend, and 2004 Judo Olympian, Dr. Rhadi Ferguson, says it this way: *"You can't do general population shit and get to the top of the mountain."* The top one percent of the one percent of achievers are very restrictive on who they allow in their inner circle. I charge you to do the same.

As I journey forward, something else I learned is to be careful who you get advice from. For years, I have hired attorneys, accountants, and other professionals, paying them in the thousands for what I thought was expert advice, only to be in the middle of a bankruptcy, or a deal gone bad, and find out I was ill advised. So, know what your team of experts know, better than they do. Understand me; I'm not advising you to do their job. Hire as many attorneys and other advisors as needed for your given field, but never let them be the last word. Your ass is on the line, along with your money and your reputation, so make all final decisions, and sign all checks yourself. Many people, even those practicing a certain thing, have no idea on how to make you rich.

Trust me, they are just guessing. So, learn to trust your gut or that inner voice.

Be the best listener in the room. Lots of people love to talk and be heard. I'm even guilty of it at times, but when my money is on the line, I create a sonic ear for details. I can recall the most mundane parts of the conversation. It is vital when building and fostering both new and old relationships. If you're married, or even if you've ever dated someone, you may have used this skill. Master it, and you will become the most popular person you know. All people want and need to be heard. My daughter, Spirit, has a way of getting me to practice this at my best; and like business, all relationships are about being heard.

You're the boss, so own it. Manifesting greatness requires confidence, and your team depends upon your ability to make decisions quickly. Being afraid will only stifle you from taking the necessary risk for growth. The devil preys upon the weak and indecisive, and your competitors are leaving it all out there. So, be first. I am typically on an island by myself, but I have found myself in great company. People thought Einstein, Thomas Edison, and even George Washington Carver were crazy, before their brilliance proved otherwise. Women, like Madame CJ Walker, Diane Hendricks, and

Oprah Winfrey, were overlooked, underestimated, and written off, right before they blazed a trail of success. Yes, I am a man to be measured in such company, and so are you, but I'm not here to convince you, only to provide guidance through my own lessons. So, stand tall, and be audacious in your creativity and dreams. Whether it be in business or in your personal life, you are the boss—so, manifest it.

Chapter 9

Evolution

"In the individual accomplishments of each man lies the success or failure of the group as a whole. The success of the group as a whole is the basis for any tradition which we many create. In such traditions lies the sense of discipleship and the inspiration which serves as a guide for those who come after, so that each man's job is not his job alone but a part of a greater job whose horizons we at present can only dimly imagine, for they are beyond our view."
– Dr. Charles Drew

No limit zone

There a special place I go when things seem to not be going as planned. It's an amazing place that only a few know about. Membership is super exclusive and all of us there often wonder why. Everything about this place is better than any other place we've ever been. Thinking clear is the norm. Questioning everything is understood and expected, but the best thing about this place is it's a worry free zone. Around here it's called the no limit zone. It took me a long time to get here and I'm never going back. Actually I don't think I could if I wanted to. It's called that because members know there is no limit in reaching their purpose. The mindset is so completely dialed in that nothing seems impossible. I know it's hard to fathom such a place, but when you're here, it seems like such an obvious place of existence. Why else would we be created? Certainly not to be in the rat race of life, living paycheck to paycheck. Definitely not for materialistic wealth, and even when the discussion about family comes up, we all know we were not born just to establish family. So why does each of us exist? Well, my belief is so that we can create perfection. Some believe perfection is an impossibility, but I see perfection every day. I notice how the earth revolves around the sun, and the moon around the earth. I pay attention to how the earth maintains its gravitational pull, and how the oxygen level stays perfectly mixed. There are more examples if we choose to see them. In the no limits zone each member understands that when we each play a part and connect with harmony, in sync with each other, life will change and our existence will be noticeably different. You see the devil once had me confused, upset, and wondering what it was all about, and now I know no limits.

I don't want to miss the opportunity to provide some *how tos* and *what's next*.

Google defines evolution in the following:

noun: progress
Forward or onward movement toward a destination.
"The darkness did not stop my progress."
synonyms:
forward movement, advance, going, progression, headway, passage "Boulders made progress difficult."

Advance or development toward a better, more complete, or more modern condition. "We are making progress toward equal rights."
synonyms:
development, advance, advancement, headway, step(s) forward, more improvement, betterment, growth "scientific progress"

Move forward or onward in space or time. "As the century progressed, the quality of telescopes improved."
synonyms:
go, make one's way, move, move forward, go forward, proceed, advance, go on, continue, make headway, work one's way. "They progressed slowly down the road."

Advance or develop toward a better, more complete, or more modern state. "Work on the pond is progressing."
synonyms:
develop, make progress, advance, make headway, take steps forward, move on, get on, gain ground, more improve, get better, come on, come along, make strides.

So, I find it fitting to make this my final chapter. My entire life has been an evolution of struggles and progress. It has been a challenge sometimes to define its purpose and meaning. It has been difficult to understand others that I have been placed on this journey with. I have been angry with God. I have been weary of hope and even contemplated death. I have been in the belly of hell and smelled its stench. I have seen its destruction and beastly nature. I have known its vomit and tasted its unpleasantness. I have witnessed its murder and have been moistened by its blood. I have felt its punch and fallen on my face, but persistence has been my gift in the darkness.

So, I will start with that: Be Persistent. I have already said to write out your goals, but once they are written, do the work. No one cares how hard the uphill challenges are, but they won't seem so bad once you have achieved your goal. When I speak of persistence, I mean *be so persistent that it mirrors relentlessness.* My gift from God has been that I don't quit. I have never been the smartest person in the room, but I have often been the most persistent. That gift has blossomed into amazing opportunities.

Another blessing, which I prayed for as a young child who struggled in this area, was to become a strong reader. At the time, I wanted to become a strong reader because I hated the embarrassment that came with being a poor one. I didn't know at the time that the gift of reading would open up endless possibilities. I urge you to read. Turn off the television, put down the phone, unplug from Facebook, and read. We are in a time in history where there is information on almost everything. Access to information was once the biggest difference between the *have* and *have not*. Today, the biggest difference may be who is willing or not willing to read. Now, I enjoy reading history, self-improvement, and informational books, but what I know is that the top CEOs read about sixty books a year. So, measure yourself against those who are where you want to be. Reading will change your life, and the people you spend your time with will also change.

Experience things that make you stretch yourself, perhaps even giving you a low level of discomfort. To be your best, you have to be able to rise above things that make you feel uncomfortable. It is the only way many will force themselves to meet new people or try new things. Again, one of the things I notice from many interviews I have conducted is that the most successful people are always trying new things. They are always stretching themselves. Whether it be running a marathon, fasting, or even speaking in front of a crowd of people, they do it.

Which takes me to my next point: one major reason why the most success people have had such pinnacles of achievement is because they take risk. It is a must-do type of thing. Who should believe in you more than you? Think about it from my perspective as a boss.

When someone comes to me looking for a job, I question their value. I don't mean whether they are important to the world; I mean, what thing can they help me do better or more efficiently than I am currently doing? I have doubt, because I have been sold before on a bag of wooden nickels. Being the boss that I am, those who are truly confident in what they can do, provide a service and fill a void. They rarely ask someone for a job; they simply create one for themselves. So, risk-taking is a must; in my business, I don't like using professionals who have never invested in real estate or who are afraid of risk.

Something I believe that is important to share is to learn to make decisions fast. People who are at the zenith of life do this well. Understand that the best businesses provide the fastest and best solutions for their customers. I am a business, and I provide solutions for people with housing problems. I know the best way to figure out the financial issue as it relates to buying a house or renovation concerns. I have mastered this, and quick resolution is my strong point. Whatever your business, you must be able to provide a quick solution for your market. If you are unable to do so, someone else will, and the solution they are providing may still not provide what is needed, but it may be the only option. So, be of service—solve problems.

I made a lot of mistakes over my eighteen years of investing in real estate. I really don't want you to go through all that I have, and that is one of my reasons for writing this book. Look, so many people will invest in real estate or in the financial markets without putting in the time to study. I don't mean read a book or two, although most people won't even do that; instead, they will listen to a friend or relative who invests on the side. No, I mean real study: reading, research, and seminars. If you're going to be successful in this business, you must immerse yourself. I have researched and paid tens of thousands of dollars to understand best how to protect myself. *I've learned how to set up all types of trust*: land trust, personal property trust, and living trust. If you are buying real estate, or anything in your name, in this *quick-to-litigate* time, you are already losing. It's time to stop playing business, and become one.

I would also caution you about traditional financing from banks. I know there will be many who will now pause, but I am confident in my position because I understand banks and banking. So, before you discount my concerns, study up on the Federal Reserve, founded in 1913, under the leadership of Woodrow Wilson. The Federal Reserve is not owned or operated by the federal government but by eight private families: Rockefeller; Goldman Sachs; Lehman; Kuhn and Loeb - all of the US Rothschilds and Rothchilds of Paris and London;

Lazard; Warburgs of Hamburg; and Israel Moses Seif of Rome. The system of money or lending is controlled by what is known by few as the four horsemen of banking. This system spends billions of dollars each year lobbying congress. They are only outspent by two other industries: food and drugs. Once I came upon this knowledge, it changed the game for me. You see, this entire banking system lends money to our government, and the government then taxes its citizens. So, hopefully now, if you wondered why the government bailed out the banks, it's a little clearer now. So, Wall Street got bailed out, and Main Street got set out—set out of their homes, and set out of the discussion for real regulation of a top heavy system. I still have some loans, but my goal is to borrow no more from traditional banks; hopefully, you won't either. The system is one that is doing us more harm than good. Did you know that, with most foreclosures, the bank has already been paid back, or has written off the bad debt? Often times, the bad debt is sold for less than what is owed, and the shortage is written off. The bank, or investor, who buys the debt, goes after the homeowner for the full amount that was owned to the original lender, even though they only paid pennies on the dollar for the bad paper. They already have instant equity, but they still take the home and resell it at market value. Sounds pretty crummy, right? Well, there is more: if they don't make more than what was originally owed, they go after the homeowner with a deficiency judgment. You see, that is a system of greed, and one will struggle to build wealth or happiness in a system like that. That's a system only designed to take, not serve. So, for me to be my best, I have decided to not follow the bandwagon. I want to revolutionize housing so that everyone who has a job can at least own a home. So, I recently became a Certified Affordable Housing Provider allowing me to finance those of you who can't qualify for a traditional mortgage. You should not have to rent if you want to own. The devil doesn't like when I talk like this and tell his secrets, so please don't let all this information go to waste. Spread the knowledge, and learn to invest instead of spending. The system will bow down to the people if the people take control of their power. As I have said, I study history and people. Elijah Muhammad showed us how with a third grade education, if one studies, she can become a master of business commerce. The Amish have shown us that keeping it simple can oftentimes be the best way to maintain control. If you ever want to regain your power, you must first change, and reprogram all the false teachings. I believe in being a boss, being a business, and being global. When you change your thinking to this type, in order to become a boss and a business, the world will look different. You will no longer play the credit score game—you won't need to.

When you prove there is a service that the world needs, it will pay you for it. You become, in the words of Booker T. Washington, *indispensable.*

The ancestors' spirits have pulled me from the hell fire. Written goals have defined my meaning and purpose. Listening has given me understanding of my wife, and made my journey one of exhilaration of exploration. Speaking life has given me a connection to the Creator and a universal order to all my requests. My inner circle provides me with hope that I, too, will accomplish my dreams, and my *why* is divine and in direct correlation with my power and purpose. I illuminate the stench and poor taste to perfect my weaknesses and firm up my will. I take time to think and measure myself often, not to be caught drifting and wasting my precious gifts. The ancestors' spirits (*Reginald F Lewis, John H Johnson)* have pulled me from the hellfire, refreshed my face with water, infused me with confidence, and made me the boss. I will be a billionaire by 2030, and the world will know I am truly back from hell—and the devil didn't win.

About The Author

Gary Rahman has owned and been managing residential and commercial real estate for the last eighteen years. He has expertise in architecture and financial planning, enabling him and his many companies to be a full-service property and investment management provider for a diverse clientele.

Gary has always been committed to changing communities. His many companies are engaged in developing housing for low to medium income families and renovating formerly abandoned buildings in order to improve the landscape and change the dynamics of urban neighborhoods. He is also a certified affordable housing provider and provides financing for potential home owners that can't qualify for traditional financing.

Gary is the managing member or Principal in several companies. Gary's roots in property management began in hotel management, where he developed a dedication to service that is evident in his customer relations today.

With an educational background in both architecture and financial planning, Gary combines the sound knowledge and skills needed to provide in-depth consulting to his clients. Gary is also a trained motivational speaker, business coach and radio host of Connection. Two of Gary's main goals are to create single handedly the most homeowners and millionaires the world has known.

In memory of Emily Yvonne Gudger aka Ma

"Legacy is our opportunity to live forever. It is what we do today to improve the lives of others that will determine whether our legacy is long or short, good or bad. We all have a gift to share, but for some reason, often times, it never gets released."

Gary Rahman, *Legacy*

56660580R00080

Made in the USA
Middletown, DE
23 July 2019